DECISION AND DISSENT

DECISION
AND
DISSENT

With Halsey at Leyte Gulf

CARL SOLBERG

NAVAL INSTITUTE PRESS
ANNAPOLIS, MARYLAND

Printed in the United States of America
on acid-free paper ∞

02 01 00 99 98 97 96 95   9 8 7 6 5 4 3 2

First printing

LIBRARY OF CONGRESS CATALOGING-IN-PUBLICATION DATA

Solberg, Carl, 1915–
    Decision and dissent : with Halsey at Leyte Gulf / Carl
Solberg.
        p.   cm.
    Includes bibliographical references and index.
    ISBN 1-55750-791-0 (acid-free paper)
    1. Solberg, Carl, 1915–   . 2. World War, 1939–1945—Naval
operations, American. 3. World War, 1939–1945—Campaigns—
Pacific Area. 4. World War, 1939–1945—Campaign, Philippines
—Leyte Island. 5. Philippine Sea, Battles of the, 1944. 6. Leyte
Island (Philippines)—History, Military. 7. World War, 1939–1945
—Personal narratives, American. 8. World War, 1939–1945—
Military intelligence—Pacific Area. 9. Halsey, William Frederick,
1882–1959. 10. MacArthur, Douglas, 1880–1964. 11. Intelligence
officers—United States—Biography. 12. United States. Navy—
Biography. I. Title.
D774.P5S65   1995
940.54'26—dc20   95-12402

CONTENTS

DECISION AND DISSENT

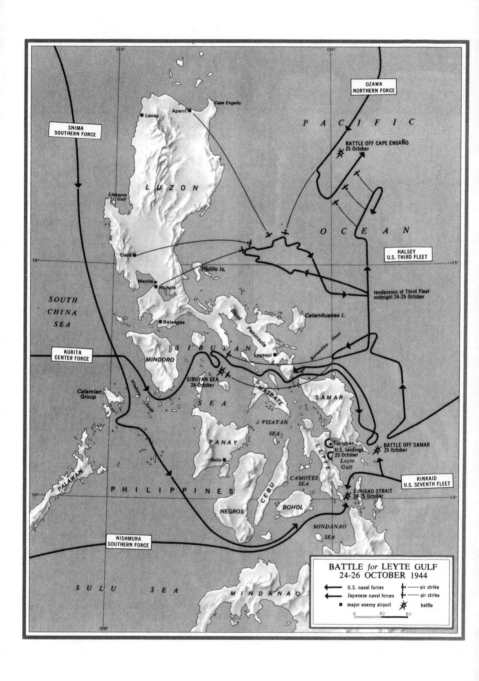

BATTLE for LEYTE GULF
24-26 OCTOBER 1944

CROSSING THE POPE'S LINE

WE WERE A LITTLE BAND of NAVAL RESERVISTS, SNATCHED from civilian life, given a smattering of training at Quonset Point, near Newport, Rhode Island, and then shipped out to the Pacific war in the summer of 1942. A cub writer on *Time* magazine, I had volunteered for flight training but failed to make the grade. "We're prolonging your life," said the board of examiners at Brooklyn's Floyd Bennett Field, and waved me off to a category called "Aviation Volunteer Specialist," which is how I got into this crowd bound for nonflying duty out where the war was. Most in our party were assigned to the Navy's South Pacific command, which had just made a first landing against fierce Japanese opposition at Guadalcanal and Tulagi. A few of us went on to Melbourne and then Brisbane, Australia, where we reported to what was left of the old Asiatic fleet, now the tiny naval component of Douglas MacArthur's Southwest Pacific command.

We were Air Combat Intelligence (ACI) officers, something new in the Navy and mystifying to those who examined our orders at Brisbane. Intelligence as such, keeping track of the enemy, its capabilities and intentions, was as old as the wooden-ship navy. But air combat intelligence sprang from the new urgencies of war waged in the air. Aviation buffs of the Yale Flying Unit of World War I fame had been to the Battle of Britain and seen how men, somewhat older, had been assigned to

Royal Air Force squadrons, lived with the airmen, briefed them before missions, interrogated them on their return, then flashed the action report to higher command. These RAF officers, informed, tactful, supportive, and presumably endowed with maturer judgment, became the model for the Navy's ACIs in World War II.

At first the Yale tinge gave the ACI project something of an elitist coloration. Artemus ("Di") Gates, the assistant secretary of the Navy for air, on leave from J. P. Morgan, and his old comrades from 1917, Lester Armour and Harry Davison, got the program started. Tom Gates, Di Gates's nephew, was one of the first ACIs, and himself later served as secretary of the Navy and defense under President Eisenhower.

Those who reported to the South Pacific command in Noumea immediately saw action. Lt. Cdr. John Endicott Lawrence, one of our best, joined the first Marine squadrons at Guadalcanal's Henderson air strip just as the Japanese, having sunk our cruisers in deadly night battles, were about to drive our forces out of the Solomons. Night after night Lawrence dived for his foxhole as battleships rained 14-inch shells on the shore encampments. Next morning he would get radioed word from Australian coconut planters further north — coastwatchers, we called them — of Japanese bombers winging south from their big base at Rabaul. He would hand these reports to the Marine fighter pilots in time for them to get airborne and intercept at least some of the attacking enemy. Then, as the pilots brought their bullet-ridden Wildcats back on the metal mat that passed for a runway, he extracted their stories and shot the word fast to Commander Aircraft Solomons (COMAIRSOLS) on the next island.

But in the Southwest Pacific it was different, not the Navy's war at all. To get there we crossed a veritable wall, the "Pope's Line," that divided the South Pacific from the theater created expressly for General MacArthur. The hero of Bataan and Corregidor had been spirited out of the Philippines to Australia.

Once there, he had vowed grandly, "I shall return," even though he had all he could do keeping the Japanese from overrunning his front in New Guinea, defended chiefly at that point by Aussies.

Since there were practically no Navy squadrons in the Southwest Pacific in 1942, after a few days we were assigned to various headquarter staffs. Although assigned to the naval command then called COMSOWESPAC, a few of us were told to report to the Allied Air Intelligence Center under MacArthur's newly arrived aviation chief, Lt. Gen. George Kenney.

The entire Southwest Pacific command was housed in Brisbane's one tall building, an eight-story structure that belonged to an insurance company. On the top floor sat MacArthur himself. On the fifth floor were his naval subordinates. And on the fourth floor were General Kenney and his supporting staff, as well as our little complement of naval reservists. A single elevator served us all, including MacArthur, whose four-star Daimler stood idling daylong at the curb outside should the general descend to enter it.

When he did descend, he had to make his way through an extremely small lobby. One day a soldier stationed himself at the foot of the elevator. As the general emerged, the GI boldly accosted the hero. "General," he said, "I've always wanted to meet you." MacArthur paused to shake his hand. The soldier said, "And general, I've always wanted your picture." Thereupon MacArthur reached in his pocket, handed him a photograph, and strode to the waiting Daimler.

In 1942 Australia still predominated at Brisbane headquarters, and I had reason to be grateful for it. From my chief, Squadron Leader R. H. Wreford, a Sydney executive who had served with the RAF in England, I learned the rudiments of air intelligence. I learned to sift the heavy flow of dispatches from both South and Southwest Pacific and to sharpen the analysis of the action reports we prepared daily, even hourly, for General Kenney. Before long, Wreford permitted me to make visits to the forward area. (When I excitedly reported egging a Catalina skipper into a vain bombing try to sink the nightly Japanese sub running supplies from Rabaul to Lae, he penciled across the paper: "Better that Fifth Air Force deals with these supply subs when they are stationary at Lae.") I visited B-17 and B-25 squadrons and took down their stories. In an outdoor shower at Dobodura I ran into Maj. Carl Hustad of the 43rd Heavy Bombardment Group after a mission against Rabaul—he and I had been baptized in the same water in Minneapolis. I hung out with Army air intelligence captain Buck Wiss, the ex–New Jersey utilities exec whose stripside generator at Port Moresby bore the legend, "New Guinea Power & Light." I lost my good friend Capt. Bill Graham, peacetime political writer for the *Omaha World Herald,* when his B-24 crashed at Salamaua.

I rejoiced in the Fifth Air Force's great coup of March 1943 when B-25s, having practiced skip-bombing for just such a moment, used a code-breaking tip to intercept a convoy carrying an entire Japanese infantry division from Rabaul to Lae and, boring in at masthead height, sank twelve transports and four escorting destroyers by bouncing bombs against their sides.

For a long time MacArthur brooked no slightest variance in the Pope's Line dividing the Navy's South Pacific command from his. When Halsey's forces clawed out of the Guadalcanal mire in early 1943 and prepared to slog further up the Solomons, they ran into this ridiculous boundary, which ran right through the South Pacific's next objective, the island of New Georgia, just north of Guadalcanal. Before the assault, agreement had to be worked out with the olympian general: MacArthur was proclaimed overall commander, Halsey was said to be in "tactical" command, and MacArthur would issue the communiqués. And florid they were. Ours reported matter-of-factly, "29 planes bombed Munda without opposition except A.A." As broadcast from MacArthur headquarters this became "29 planes pressed through heavy A/A fire to drop bombs at Munda, setting fires that were visible for 60 miles."

Of course there were those at Admiral Nimitz's headquarters back in Hawaii who could see that MacArthur's demarcation line couldn't last much longer. Pouring out of America's shipyards were warships of all types and sizes, including lots of fast aircraft carriers. The planners at Pearl Harbor were already deploying them in the central Pacific and were bent now on spreading destruction on the Japanese far beyond MacArthur's line. Their leader was Adm. Jack Towers, who had spearheaded the carrier-building program in Washington and was now at Nimitz's right hand as Commander Aircraft Pacific (COM-AIRPAC) pushing their use. First of all, said George ("Wing") Pepper, chief of Towers's ACIs gathering strength at Pearl Harbor, we had to find out about the air war on the far side of the line.

And so it was that Capt. Andrew McCollum, my boss as newly arrived Navy intelligence chief in Brisbane, complying with the request for an officer from the Southwest Pacific, tapped me as the most footloose junior on his roster to fly across the line and report to Wing Pepper and his pool of ACIs.

In Hawaii I was greeted like a Marco Polo arriving from unknown China, debriefed like a prisoner of war, lent briefly to Nimitz's staff, and after supplying twenty-five pages anatomizing MacArthur country, given the chance at last to go where the action was—the South Pacific. That landed me back in Noumea to rejoin John Lawrence with whom I had crossed the Pacific in 1942 and who was now back at South Pacific headquarters in charge of a sizable pool of ACI officers. His style was to dispatch newly arrived ACIs to temporary duty with air units in the forward areas. He sent me to report to COMAIRSOLS, at the time Marine Maj. Gen. Ralph Mitchell, located at the newly captured base at Munda, New Georgia.

There I learned from Lt. Frank Bowen, the chief ACI, that I was once again to be a staff officer. I might lodge in a sodden tent with Marine fighter pilot Maj. Frank Porter and Fighter Command's ACI, Lt. Joe Bryan. But my post would be at a field desk in a sweltering Quonset hut beside the fighter strip, collecting, sifting, and relaying COMAIRSOLS's daily action reports to Halsey and others. And each day I'd walk to the general's heavily sandbagged command post and recount for the general's morning meeting what our forces had done the day before and what they aimed to do that day. At day's end we would saunter slowly past the hut of Fighter Command's Virginian chief, Col. William Oscar Brice—and wheel fast as whippets when he called us to share his evening Southern Comfort. The air and sea onslaught from Rabaul had begun to abate, and our nocturnal concerns had shifted from stopping Tokyo Express destroyer runs to hunting down troop-carrying barges in jungle coves. What now kept us awake nights was the pesky bomber with the noisy engine, Washing-machine Charlie, who flew insolently low and dropped bombs called daisy-cutters that went off on impact and sent shrapnel flying through our tents. It was at Munda that Joe Bryan, standing beside our foxhole and editing his biblical lines as if he, not I, had endured similar New Guinea nights, cracked, "Never had the Solomons in all their glory a raid like one of these."

From muddy Munda our forces moved on up the Solomons. In a spectacular bit of leap-frogging past bristling Japanese bases, Halsey brought off a landing on an unoccupied patch of coast on Bougainville, within easy striking distance of Rabaul. Stronger now and getting stronger, we sent up swarms of fighters to escort masses of bombers thundering northward to plaster Rabaul. And on Bougainville we lived better. The site was laid out on level volcanic sand so that four inches of rain— and it rained up to six times a day—drained promptly away into the fabulously porous soil beneath us. We still ate Marine chow—dehydrated eggs for breakfast, split wieners and sauerkraut for dinner. But now we could duck away for dusk dips at the black-sand beach, and rinse off afterward under tipover buckets of water called showers.

Months passed. Wisconsin's Joe McCarthy, yes, Marine Capt.

Joseph N. McCarthy, arrived at the field desk next to mine to replace Capt. Don Stauffer, the Princeton English prof who had remarked of one of my dispatches to Noumea, "Carl, you have no style." Bryan left, Frank Bowen left, Porter returned for a second hitch. In honor of his fellow Virginian, Colonel Brice, Bryan hung a Confederate flag on our tent over the legend "COMCONFORSOLS"—that is, Commander Confederate Forces Solomon Islands. Now we hung a mocking banner, "South Pacific Headquarters McCarthy for Senator." (Little did we know that Joe would suddenly receive mysterious orders to stateside, enabling him to run for the Senate in Wisconsin that fall.) Art Chamberlain, a resourceful ex-legislator from Alaska, moved into our tent and won us over by rigging a second tent above it and thereby practically air-conditioning our pad.

Halsey leapfrogged again, this time to Green Island, and Rabaul—Fortress Rabaul—was left behind. Now our four-

At our Bougainville tent in early 1944, which still sports the Confederate flag raised at Munda for our Virginian colonel, William Oscar Brice. Marine Capt. Joe McCarthy surveys our derisive banner, "McCarthy for U.S. Senator".

engine bombers could challenge Truk, an even bigger base so much further north that it wasn't really in the South Pacific at all. I lost another friend, Bill Conway, on an early mission, and we anxiously awaited the first B-24 sent up to photograph Truk. On his return the pilot flashed a red light. The ambulance was waiting. But he got down all right on our fighter strip. And when our jeep caught up at plane-side, the 20-year-old captain had already hopped out and was kissing the ground.

One day the rest of us were stretched out on our cots for the noon siesta when Chamberlain walked in. "Solberg," he said, "you're mentioned in dispatches." Sure enough, the orders said return to Noumea. I'd been 15 months in the islands. I'd seen five tentmates off one after another to better places. Now it was my turn.

In Noumea John Lawrence told me that Admiral Halsey, his South Pacific job done, was going to sea. He and his exec, John Marshall, were going to sea with him. And I was to go along. It was Marshall who later told me that sometime in the spring of 1944 John Lawrence had gotten wind that the Third Fleet, which had been established on paper in March 1943, was to be activated, and Halsey, freed from shore duties, would lead it as the striking force of Admiral Nimitz's Pacific fleet.

John was determined that ACI be represented when that happened. When he learned that Halsey was going on an important mission to Pearl Harbor, he wangled a place in the plane. He hardly knew Admiral Halsey at the time, but managed to sit next to him and then filled him with the value of ACI. The result was that when the Third Fleet staff was made up, the intelligence section included three ACIs in addition to two fleet intelligence officers. Capt. Mike Cheek headed up the intelligence staff, and Lt. Harris Cox, who had been his assistant at Noumea, was the other fleet intelligence specialist. There was also Cdr. Gil Slonim's radio decoding unit but they were quite independent.

Admiral Halsey pins the Legion of Merit on Lt. Cdr. John E. Lawrence, head of Third Fleet's Air Combat Intelligence contingent and
a resourceful member of Halsey's "dirty tricks department."

I was the third and juniormost ACI, chosen because Lawrence—remembering my experience on the other side of
the Line and mindful that the Navy would now have to work
closely with MacArthur in retaking the Philippines—thought
I'd be useful. Sure enough, they sent me right away to get Mac-
Arthur's people to make aerial photographs of Third Fleet's first
invasion target, Palau.

We had almost no charts or information about this island
group in the western Carolines: the Japanese had kept them,
along with their other bases in the mandated islands, quaran-
tined from the rest of the world. Fast carrier strikes in the Carolines in early 1944 had produced our first glimpse of the Palaus.
But systematic photo reconnaissance was needed to make the

maps required for invasion purposes. And such photos would
have to come from the Southwest Pacific.

MacArthur's advances westward along the New Guinea coast
had just about brought Palau within range of his forward bases.
But first I had to stop at General Kenney's headquarters in Brisbane. Some at Noumea might have thought I was young for
my mission. But they should have noted General Kenney's
operations officer. He was a red-headed flier, a West Pointer
named Frank Gideon, a chicken colonel who had yet to see 30
and may have been nearer 25. He listened to my plea and said it
could be done. Low-level photos of beaches were out of the
question. But Fifth Air Force had some high-flying, long-legged
F-5s, which were twin-engine, specially equipped P-38 Light-
ning fighters. Staging through newly won coral strips at Wakde
and Biak, these planes could and would do the job, he said.
With this for a starter, I loaded a case of scotch in my duffel bag
and headed for New Guinea. I flew past the fought-over places
like Lae, Salamaua, and Finschafen, on to Nadzab, the newly
won forward command center at Hollandia, and on for a look
at the strip at Biak, which was still under enemy shellfire. Back
at Nadzab, I visited the Sixth Photographic Group, where I saw
with my own eyes that our Palau mission was listed on the as-
signment board.

Since the early days at Guadalcanal, ACIs had an officer-
messenger service to disseminate intelligence documents to all
South Pacific commands as quickly as possible. We found that
our network had far faster delivery than material sent through
the regular communications center. Realizing the importance
of expediting delivery of the invasion photographs, I arranged,
with the help of a bottle of scotch from my duffel bag, to
have two sets of the photographs made — one to be forwarded
through the proper channels and the other to be sent direct to
ACI Third Fleet in Pearl Harbor by officer messenger. I then
proceeded to cover our officer-messenger route to Hawaii,
meeting the head of each ACI unit and extracting a promise,

with the help of a bottle of scotch, to speed the pictures on their way when they came through. The last stop was Hickam Field, Honolulu, where I left the telephone number of Third Fleet's ACI office. One day in July we saw in the dispatches that Fifth Air Force had photographed Palau. One week later the phone message came from Hickam Field that our package was there. Before John Marshall and I drove over to pick up the package he called the photo interpreters and mapmakers. It was about five in the afternoon when we delivered the pictures to the photo interpreters. They worked steadily through that first night and on until the maps and charts for the invasion were completed. A month later the official set of pictures arrived, but they made no stir. By then they were old hat.

This expedition led to another. In August I flew back to the Southwest Pacific, my mission this time to make sure that fighting units of Third Fleet would get all possible combat information from MacArthur country as they went into battle.

By this time the Southwest Pacific had generated a lot of intelligence material. Captain McCollum, my old boss, now presided over a Seventh Fleet Intelligence Center of 150 officers. We arranged to have charts, maps, photographs, bulletins, and reports shipped to our forward bases, first Manus Island and later Ulithi, for transfer to the fast carriers. Of particular interest was their elaborate guerrilla network in the Philippines. We knew how valuable coastwatchers had been for our airmen in the South Pacific, and we wanted to assure pilots that friendly folks on shore stood ready to rescue downed airmen. Also, General Kenney's crews were now operating long-range reconnaissance flights over the western Pacific, and it was essential that they and our force at sea were quite literally on the same wavelength. Third Fleet commands were made addressees for flash reports sent by Fifth Air Force and Seventh Fleet searchers as they probed deep into enemy waters.

On September 4 I boarded the admiral's flagship *New Jer-*

sey for the first time just as Third Fleet's Striking Force sortied from Manus harbor. And what a walloper of a fleet I joined: instead of the single aircraft carrier *Enterprise* that Halsey had commanded after Pearl Harbor, here were sixteen new fast carriers mounting 1,000 attack planes; instead of the waddling old battlewagons sunk at Pearl Harbor, six new fast battleships including the superbattleship *New Jersey;* and spread out in the crowded anchorage at Manus, a hundred transports and supporting vessels that would convoy 40,000 troops to Third Fleet's first invasion target, Palau, just 10 days later.

Halsey made no secret of his distaste for invading Palau. He wanted to bypass the place and go straight for the Philippines. He was the redoubtable Halsey, known to practically every American as their most combative naval commander. He had been held ashore at Noumea since his early task-force exploits because his type of fighting leadership was precisely what was needed to pull together the battered, shaken Marines, sailors, and soldiers in the South Pacific, instill in them the confidence and resolve to hold the Japanese and fight them to a standstill, and then lead his men to victory.

And now, when Halsey put to sea, all who served knew that his powerful Third Fleet was headed for action. His armada of 100 carriers, battleships, cruisers, and destroyers would range far beyond the amphibious force putting troops ashore at Palau. They would sail west to the Philippines, west to Asia, north to the gates of Japan itself, spreading destruction in the enemy's sealanes, disrupting vital supply lines, smashing ports and airfields, challenging the Japanese navy to come out and fight.

The command setup requires a word of explanation. As Admiral Nimitz deployed his forces, Third Fleet under Halsey and Fifth Fleet under Admiral Spruance, the victor of Midway, took turns leading the attack forces. The ships and men they led were the same. But while one led one assault, the other was back at base planning the next one. Spruance's Fifth Fleet had

just invaded and captured the Marianas. Halsey's Third Fleet
was now to seize the Carolines, then provide strategic support
for MacArthur's landings in the Philippines. After that, Fifth
Fleet would take Okinawa, while Halsey's Third Fleet staff
planned the assault, again with MacArthur, on Japan itself.
Back in Hawaii Halsey had laid plans to lead Third Fleet's
mighty Striking Force attacking Japanese strongholds all
around the western Pacific, which would soften up Japanese resistance to MacArthur's return to the Philippines. But there was
an additional proviso in Nimitz's directive to Halsey. If at any
point Halsey's marauding would bring forth the Japanese fleet,
then his first priority, overriding even strategic support for Mac-
Arthur's landings, would be to annihilate the enemy ships. This
directive was a direct consequence of the American experience
in the fight for the Marianas a few months before. The invasion
of the Marianas, 1,200 miles from Tokyo itself, had been a challenge sufficient to call forth the Japanese fleet. In that great
confrontation, known as the Battle of the Philippine Sea, the
entire Japanese fleet came out to meet our forces. Our fast carrier force met and decisively defeated them, our fliers shooting down some 500 of their best carrier pilots in what they
called the "Marianas Turkey Shoot." But our carriers were held
back from pursuing the beaten enemy force because, as Admiral Spruance read his directive from Nimitz, *his* overriding
duty was to safeguard the troops going ashore on Saipan,
Tinian, and Guam. In this way the Japanese fleet escaped what
would have been a knockout.

Uppermost in Halsey's mind as he prepared to go to sea again
was the less-than-conclusive outcome of the June battle. Moreover, senior members of his staff, aboard Fifth Fleet carriers as
observers, had witnessed this outcome and came away resolved
that when Third Fleet went out to fight no Japanese at all could
be allowed to escape. Halsey and his men worked up the plan
in Hawaii for the coming campaign, drawing up schemes for

Third Fleet's mighty Task Force 34, the battle line of dreadnoughts formed to ensure that no Japanese ships would escape, never saw action at the Leyte battle. Later, when Halsey carried the attack to Japan's shores, battlewagons (trailed by a couple of cruisers) bombarded the steelworks at Kamaishi.

sending the Navy's massed striking power far and wide in enemy waters. Halsey then talked it out with Nimitz and this became the new directive.

Leading the charge would be the formidable fast carrier Task Force 38 under Adm. Marc Mitscher, Halsey's old top airman in the South Pacific, delivering pulverizing air strikes against Luzon, Formosa, Okinawa, against Tokyo itself. But Halsey's battle plan had a new feature: Task Force 34.

In the event of a fleet action, Task Force 34 would be formed at Halsey's order from the big battleships and cruisers otherwise serving as antiaircraft gunships protecting the fast carriers of Task Force 38. Halsey's own flagship, the 52,000-ton superbattleship *New Jersey,* would be a part of this force, which would be commanded by Adm. Ching Lee, the redoubtable Commander Battleships, Pacific (COMBATPAC), in *Washington.* So for the first time since Pearl Harbor the Battle Line would come back to life: *New Jersey* and sister ship *Iowa,* plus *Alabama, North Carolina, Massachusetts, South Dakota,* and *Washington,* every one of them fast as carriers and mounting nine 16-inch guns. Their task, in case of a real fleet action, would be to forge ahead, out in front of the attacking carrier force, to be in position to pounce on and finish off "cripples" so that these enemy ships could not get home and return to fight again.

No sooner had we departed Manus than Halsey directed Ching Lee to form Task Force 34 and put the big ships through their paces. It was an eye-opening sight for me as our huge ship and *Iowa* paired off with the other four fast battlewagons and drilled in a formation never before seen in the war. For three days we drilled in Battle Line. And again, after we had joined Task Force 38 for the Palau landing and the first charge at the Philippines, when Third Fleet's fighting ships retired toward Ulithi, Admiral Lee once more formed Battle Line and sent these six great sea monsters steaming, as it seemed, nose to fantail, wheeling and countermarching briskly at the command of flag signals from Lee's quarterdeck. Morale aboard the six new dreadnoughts deployed in Task Force 34 shot sky high. The men on *New Jersey* drilled with shining eyes. Their time was at hand.

For bluewater sailors, this was their chance. By the proudest American tradition, battleships had always been top dog. More than any other instruments of armed might, they had made the United States a world power. From the 1898 victories at Santiago and Manila Bay, battleships proclaimed America's con-

quering might in two oceans. After World War I battleships became the official measure of America's martial standing when
the Treaty of Washington set the 5:5:3 ratio for naval powers—
fifteen of these capital ships for America and Britain, twelve for
Japan.

These dreadnoughts were burly monsters, armed and armored like no other instruments of warfare on earth. But they
were slow, and when the next world conflagration broke out
President Roosevelt, even before he called on U.S. war plants
to build a seemingly impossible 50,000 planes a year, set an
equally challenging goal for naval design: a force of new battleships that could deliver their mighty blows at a speed equal to
that of those trim little greyhounds, the destroyers—35 knots.

It was a tall order, and the Navy did its best. The first big
ships built in the big rearmament program, *North Carolina*
and *Washington,* and the four battlewagons of the *South Dakota*
class that followed, attained speeds of 26 knots—much faster
than the waddling old battlewagons of World War I. All the
authorities are not on agreement on this, but those of us who
sailed on the superbattleships laid down after the start of World
War II and before Pearl Harbor believe they met FDR's mark.
These were the four great ships of the *Iowa* class, including our
flagship *New Jersey, Missouri,* and *Wisconsin.*

Of the fast battleships that arrived in the Pacific before the
supers, a few saw some old-fashioned slam-bang action. In fact
Lee's flagship *Washington* was the only battleship to sink another battleship in the war thus far. It happened in a night
action off Guadalcanal on November 16, 1943. Up to this time
the Japanese had been winning these sudden, deadly night battles. On this occasion they were trying to land an entire division of troops on Guadalcanal and retake the island. The opening night they surprised our cruisers in the narrow waters off
Savo Island and sank two of them. Next day in the seesaw fight
our side struck back. Planes from Henderson Field and the carrier *Enterprise* caught the Japanese transports nearing their goal,

sank six ships laden with troops, and forced the other four to beach on Guadalcanal's northeast coast.

The following night it was Lee's turn. As darkness fell he led his six-ship force forward just south of Guadalcanal. The enemy had lost some ships, too, and were not up to parading past our beachhead and raining 14-inch shells on our airstrip as they had done a month before. But they were spoiling for a fight, confident that in night fighting they excelled.

This time the Americans had certain advantages. Both Lee's flagship and its sister ship *South Dakota* boasted 16-inch guns, bigger than anything the Japanese had in the area. And *Washington* had important new radar, not the search radar that never seemed to pick out the cruisers and destroyers darting out from the cover of Savo Island until it was too late. What Lee had aboard *Washington* was the Navy's latest fire-control radar for his main and secondary batteries. Not even *South Dakota* had that, just an earlier, inferior type.

All the same, the Japanese struck first. Suddenly their warships blinked on searchlights and caught the four destroyers in Lee's van in their glare. Taking aim at these targets, within minutes they reduced two of them to blazing wrecks. *South Dakota,* coming up to the right of the burning destroyers, found itself silhouetted against the night sky—an inviting target for Japanese gunners by now no more than 5,000 yards away. At such close quarters they couldn't miss. And at such short range the trajectory of their shells was flat so that the forty-two shells that ripped into *South Dakota* riddled the ship's superstructure. They destroyed the ship's communications, wiped out Radar Plot, and knocked out four of the ship's old fire-control radars. Unable even to report its plight to Lee, *South Dakota* withdrew, with thirty-eight killed and sixty wounded.

Washington, as it happened, had swung just far enough to the left so that it passed to the far side of the burning destroyers—throwing rafts over the side to destroyer men adrift in the water as it passed—and stayed invisible to the enemy. But visible on

Washington's fire-control radar were plenty of enemy targets, and the biggest of all was a blip no more than 6,000 yards away. Exactly at midnight Lee opened fire on what he was pretty sure was a Japanese battleship. To *Washington's* gunnery officer, a mere 6,000 yards was "body-punching range." His first salvo straddled the target, the second was a hit, the third, he said, was "right on." Racked by explosions, the enemy ship turned to flee, but *Washington* kept pouring it on. The secondary battery of five-inchers scored forty hits. Tracers from *Washington's* 16-inch salvos cast a red glow in the sky. Finally, at 11,000 yards, *Washington* broke off, having fired seventy-three rounds from its 16-inch rifles, marking the end of what proved to be the battleship *Kirishima.*

At 0040 Lee withdrew in a tremendous, shuddering turn. It took the big ship two minutes to reverse course. At 26 knots *Washington* set up an enormous bow wave, and Lt. Bill Powers atop the mainmast in Fire Control Two had to hold on for all he was worth. The vibration was terrific. Hanging on to his perch, said Powers, was "like sitting on top of a pogo stick." Withdrawal was none too soon — torpedoes fired by the Japanese exploded in the ship's wake as it made its mighty turn. Next morning Powers found the deck around the five-inch mounts littered with shell casings. And looking up, he saw a hole in the ship's bedspring radar antenna — the only hit incurred by *Washington* in the night's engagement.

So there was no question that these 41,000-tonners could shoot and kill. But for size and above all speed, the superbattleships — the *Iowa* class — outclassed them. Essentially, the 52,000-ton supers attained their record speeds by reason of their size, or more precisely, their greatly increased length. Of course these four ships also packed within them the most powerful engineering plants ever installed in battleships. But their sensational new feature was their great, sweeping bow, almost unbelievably long, with a bulbous nose at the very tip that imparted some stability as well. So impossibly long was that bow that my shipmate John Marshall, on boarding *New Jersey* the first time at Pearl Harbor, took a first look forward from the flag bridge and recoiled in some alarm, thinking he was witnessing another ship bearing down for a collision.

Other tricks for driving these great ships forward included having two types of propellers at the stern, one pair of five-bladed screws inboard and a second set of four-bladed propellers slightly longer outboard. They helped damp vibration by keeping different rhythms at work in the churning sea beneath, and at the same time their great size (17 and 18½ feet tall) contributed to the ship's remarkable maneuverability—*Iowa*'s skipper claimed his ship could turn inside a destroyer.

The very fact that (like the *North Carolina*s and *South Dakota*s before them) the *Iowa*-class supers had to be capable of squeezing through the 110-foot-wide locks of the Panama Canal led to superior design. Whereas their predecessors, combining such girth with 680- and 725-foot lengths, emerged bluff and stoutish, and prone to a short, choppy roll, our far longer flagship was mercifully free from any such roll. As things turned out, our ship's 888-foot length, combined with the same 108-foot width, gave *New Jersey* and all ships of the *Iowa* class pleasing proportions and, seen in profile, splendid sweep. On balance the four *Iowa*-class supers had everything—classic 16-inch-gun offensive power, good 16-inch armor belts for protection, and speed beyond that of the Japanese superbattleships, which were heavier (63,000 tons) because they had been designed without any Panama Canal constraints. They were clearly the best ever built. They proved, as the experts said, that grace and majesty could coexist with brute force.

These ships were like cities—in fact, *New Jersey* deserved Bea Lillie's sally crossing the Atlantic in *Queen Mary:* "When does this place arrive?" On first boarding we were handed two notices. The first, "Bulletin for Officers" read as if written for a country club. After listing hours for meals served in the spacious officers' wardroom, it said, "Your room boy will collect

The superbattlewagon *New Jersey* prowls the western Pacific in 1944. The *New Jersey* served as Halsey's flagship because his penchant for improvisation required space for a large staff.

your laundry Monday and return it to you Wednesday. Laundry, cobbler services, tailoring services and haircuts are free. Medical and dental services are available to officers at all hours at Sick Bay, located at Frame 85 on the third deck." The second bulletin sounded less like a cruise director's announcements. "We cannot avoid hits below the waterline," it led off, "but we can and must see that damage from the hole is localized." Accordingly, all doors, hatches, and scuttles would be dogged tight in "Condition Zebra"—Battle Condition. But if marked "Z Modified," such openings might be undogged "for slight relaxation from Battle Condition to enable serving of meals, increased ventilation and certain head facilities during periods of Condition Zebra."

New Jersey's population already numbered 100 officers, 1,800 enlisted men. For the latter there was absolutely no privacy—troughs in the heads, four-high foldaway berths for sleeping. But *New Jersey* welcomed us aboard by making available the best accommodations. Because of his penchant for improvisation, Admiral Halsey needed a large staff, and he brought aboard some 200, including 50 officers, no fewer than 18 of them communicators, Flag country was in the tower part of the superstructure, the admiral's bridge directly under the captain's. Next below was our duty station, Flag Plot, and on the deck below were Halsey's quarters—his sleeping cabin, his office, and a room with a large oval table at which he held conferences and took his meals with senior staff. Adm. Robert Carney, his chief of staff, and other seniors had cabins on this deck. On the deck below were our junior quarters—Lawrence and Marshall together on the port side, Harris Cox and I (mine was the upper bunk) on the starboard side.

We took our meals cafeteria style in the junior officers' wardroom—fresh steaks and chops, tossed salads and not just ice cream every evening but Baked Alaska every Sunday. Cost: $35 a month, regularly reduced by a "dividend" of $5 to $10. At table I made friends with such *New Jersey* men as Capt. Frank Reagan, boss of the ship's Marine detail; Chaplain Thomas Robinson, whose years of work in the centuries-old Jesuit mission in Nagasaki were indelibly burned in my memory when I later heard where the second A-bomb was dropped; and Cdr. Mike Lefanu, who exclaimed as we watched the planes taking off from the nearby carrier, "Pity those things were invented." For indeed, there was a carrier navy and a battleship navy, and I knew that when all was said and done, we ACIs were passengers on our flagship.

In the first three months *New Jersey* steamed 36,000 miles, but not always in combat. In fact, Halsey's style as Commander Third Fleet was to race forward to strike enemy bases one day, and fall back the next day to refuel. It was this mobility that did most to protect us—and only when we stayed inshore for extended operations did we suffer losses. Sometimes the oiler group that came forward to meet us in mid-ocean would include refrigerator ships with fresh provisions, escort carriers with replacement planes and personnel, a hospital ship to take off the sick and wounded, and even a post office ship with mail. In this way we could stay at sea for months without visiting Ulithi for supplies.

Taking aboard fuel might look simple, but it was a complex operation requiring great skill. Our ship had to move in close to the tanker on parallel course until the lines could be passed between. Then hoses would be attached, and fuel pumped across the slender space between the ships. The helmsman had to keep the big ship on a steady, even course so that the lines and hoses would not part. Sometimes a tanker would service ships on both sides at once—a battleship to one side and a carrier on the other. And often the big ships passed fuel or supplies—especially movies—to destroyers on the offside at the same time. And of course the big ships often topped off the destroyers between regular fueling times.

Sometimes weather grew so severe that hoses parted and fueling had to break off. That happened in December 1944. Trying to find a safe fueling area, we succeeded in steering directly into the path of a typhoon. As the eye of the storm passed near us, I could see the cyclonic circle on the radar screen in Flag Plot.

Iowa-class battleships were known as "wet" ships, and we took a lot of water. Great waves smashed over the jutting bow, the forward turrets, even high on the bridge structure. Green water rose over the fantail, endangering the ship's floatplanes on their catapults. *New Jersey's* log states that the ship rolled 25 degrees. Belowdecks, we heard the sound of smashing glass and crockery. Shaving in his cabin, John Marshall thought he was snug and secure—until he turned to find a large filecase sliding directly at him. Whirling, he managed to hold it off until the next lurch sent it sliding back. In Flag Plot, Operations' Capt. Rollo Wilson, earphones on his head, tried vainly to keep track of all Third Fleet's storm-tossed ships: some destroyers had pumped ballast in order to take fuel and were therefore in unstable condition when the force of the storm caused fueling to break off. For two days and nights the winds howled, the rain beat down. When it was all over and Third Fleet counted its losses, we had lost three destroyers, capsized and sunk, and no fewer than 790 men lost at sea. *Cabot,* the light carrier sailing in our TG 38.2, had suffered damage when planes pulled loose and when portions of the flight deck were hurled back by the waves.

It was a disaster, a loss more grievous than any we suffered in battle—and an inglorious hour for our admiral. It took days to account for our ships, and Rollo Wilson's face was ashen as he worked over his list of ships still missing. There was a dreadful moment when the survivor captain of one foundered ship, *Hull,* came aboard, pale as a specter, wearing incongruous and obviously borrowed blues, to make his melancholy report to an anguished Halsey. Last of all, and utterly unexpected, the destroyer escort *Tabberer* of the tanker force turned up — battered, dismasted, with stacks collapsed, but somehow a survivor. Not only that, *Tabberer* had picked up some survivors from the lost destroyers. Radio gone, out of touch, *Tabberer,* we thought, was lost.

In Flag Plot we savored the story that came back to us later. It seems that *Tabberer,* jury-rigged, made its way back for heavy repairs. First stop was Manus, where a battleship riding high at anchor flashed, "What type of ship are you?" The little ship replied, "DE *Tabberer.*" That seemed a less-than-satisfying answer to *Tabberer's* signalmen. When they slogged next into Pearl Harbor another big ship looked them over and chanced to beam the same query, "What type of ship are you?" More than ready this time, the little ship winked back, "DE *Tabberer.* What type of ship are you?"

Actually, this was only the worst of the typhoons we ran into —we intercepted another later, complete with fueling group, in a bold foray into the South China Sea, but that time we fought clear unscathed. Most days, like the first morning, when I stepped out on the deck and breathed deep of the fresh air, I

felt a thrill, and it came back every day. I never tired of watching takeoffs and landings on the carriers nearby. Although
I never entered the huge turrets that dominated our decks, I
hustled up to the Fire Control Two eyrie atop the mainmast
when the big guns were unlimbered for drill after the departure
from Manus. Advised to stuff cotton in my ears, I did not hear
the two short rings of the electric bell signal. Before I knew it,
blinding tongues of flame shot out from the 68-foot-long
rifles. Each 1,900-pound projectile (the Navy does not like to
call them shells) left the muzzle at 4,500 RPM, and I could see
them as they flew toward the horizon. You felt the force of the
concussion 110 feet up. *Iowa*'s gunnery officer once said it was
rather like being hit by a slow truck wrapped in a sofa. He even
insisted that the impact of the ship's secondary batteries was
harsher: "The 5-inchers, damn them, hit you like a plank."
Working in Flag country we probably didn't realize this. The
record shows that after a barrage by the five-inchers off Okinawa *New Jersey* sent twelve men to sick bay to be treated for
flash burns, chest and nasal problems.

By the time we went to sea, all the fast battleships sprouted
so many guns they stuck out all over. Carrier admiral Frederick
Sherman went so far as to say when the big ships joined up,
"Thank goodness you're here. From now on I shan't have to
worry about providing our AA coverage." And in the next big
carrier action off Santa Cruz *South Dakota*'s guns brought
down thirty-two planes. Both *New Jersey* and *Iowa,* which always sailed in company as part of TG 38.2, mounted ten pairs
of five-inchers in their secondary battery plus sixty 40mm Bo-
fors and fifty 20mm Oerlikon machine guns. There was even a
40mm gun tub atop the No. 2 turret.

But *New Jersey* almost never had a chance to show her antiaircraft prowess because with Halsey aboard the flagship always
served as fleet guide, meaning that we sailed at the very center
of the disposition. In consequence, the ship's AA gunners almost never had a shot at low-flying bogeys closing the force for

fear of hitting one of the ships surrounding us. On the rare occasions when *New Jersey* had a clear shot, the log reported, "Ceased fire when bearing of plane endangered other vessels." In the end, the flagship shot down a grand total of just twenty enemy planes.

My post was the standup intelligence desk in Flag Plot where we stood watch between the big operations chart on one side and the admiral's transom on the other. The intelligence chief was Capt. Mike Cheek, a grizzled Annapolis grad who had been in business in the Far East and returned to duty as a reservist. Mostly he operated out of his own quarters, and sometimes looked in on our intelligence office belowdecks where three capable enlisted men kept the log of our doings. Sometimes he appeared in Flag Plot as the senior staff officer on duty but that was rare.

Keeping watch 'round the clock at our Flag Plot station were four of us. John Lawrence was our chief ACI, an astute, attractive Boston cottonbroker of impeccably Brahmin background. He often sat in at top planning sessions. Lt. John Marshall, also in his middle thirties and an investment counselor who was also a Harvard graduate, had worked at Lawrence's right hand in Noumea. Steady was the word for Marshall. Taking his turn with us was Lt. Harris Cox, a big, vastly good-natured Texan who had prospected for oil in the East Indies. I was newly promoted from lieutenant (junior grade), with additional duties in photo interpretation—which meant simply that I was custodian of the huge quantities of reconnaissance photography we received.

On September 15 Third Fleet forces invaded Palau. I remember Halsey that morning seated on his transom in Flag Plot— ostentatiously reading a paperback. I do not remember his ever doing so except this once, which I took to mean not only his complete confidence in those carrying out his orders but also his belief voiced earlier that the whole operation was really unnecessary.

Later that day the destroyer *Maddox* came alongside and took aboard two passengers. The first was Marine Gen. William Riley, Halsey's plans officer. The second, as Third Fleet's war diary records, was "Lieut. Solberg, ACI officer." Bill Riley was off to MacArthur's headquarters in Hollandia to confer with MacArthur's generals and Adm. Forrest Sherman from Nimitz's command over how to coordinate moves for the upcoming Philippines campaign. My errand was a minor but urgently specific matter: Admiral Halsey was determined within the week to launch the war's first strike against central Luzon, and MacArthur had been making noises about treating Manila as an open city. I was to go along with General Riley to find out exactly what targets our carrier planes could hit in the capital city.

MacArthur's stuffy G-2, Gen. Charles Willoughby, huffed and puffed at my appearance, but Adm. Thomas Kinkaid was helpful. And my old boss, Captain McCollum, patiently explained that while the city of Manila was not to be attacked, airfields were clearly targets. So were all the ships in the harbor as well as oil tanks lining the Pasig River. On the maps I'd brought along we carefully inked in the grid references that ACIs on the carriers could transfer to maps for their airmen. But when I wrote out these specs in a dispatch to Third Fleet McCollum took me aside. Remember, he said, this dispatch is going out over MacArthur's name; it must speak with MacArthur's voice, have MacArthur's tone. So we wrote a little preamble that went something like this: "In order to protect the brave Filipino people we are about to liberate . . . targets for carrier attacks at Manila are limited to the following. . . ."

Before I got back to my station in Flag Plot, Task Force 38 had delivered the war's first attack at Manila. The Japanese, caught as Halsey said "with their flaps down," were unable to launch a single plane until after 10 minutes of irreplaceable damage had occurred. The day's attacks left installations at the former Nichols and Clark fields in shambles. Our airmen riddled and burned 95 planes on the ground and shot down 110 aloft. They sank 11 large ships and claimed 28 more probably sunk. Photographs showed some bomb hits on the Pasig River oil tanks, and some bursts exploding in residential areas nearby. The open city lasted no longer in the Pacific than in Europe.

Mariana-based B-29s began fire-bombing Tokyo, and to retake Manila against fierce Japanese resistance MacArthur's artillery firing point-blank reduced the city's massive, ex–U.S. government buildings to rubble. In the old, walled Intramuros quarter, scarcely one stone stood upon another.

2

THE LIMITS OF OUR KNOWLEDGE

IN THE CLASSIC BUSINESS OF INTELLIGENCE, WHICH IS the collecting and interpreting of everything there is to know about one's opponent, America was miles behind the Europeans. No one—the generals, the admirals, or the university scholars of the United States—possessed anything like the intimate knowledge of the Japanese adversary in 1944 that, say, the French possessed about their German or British foes. The United States was relatively new on the world power scene, Japan even newer. Although obvious rivals, they had never fought a war. The ocean that separated them was the widest on earth. Americans, no great shakes as linguists in any case, were so far from understanding Japanese character and culture that their most widely studied interpretation of enemy thought processes, *The Chrysanthemum and the Sword,* was a work by a Columbia anthropologist, Dr. Ruth Benedict, who had never been to Japan.

But Americans are tremendous pragmatists who knew, even then, that in this century technology wins wars. By one of the most prodigious feats of the Second World War they harnessed their know-how to the needs of intelligence, bypassing the whole matter of understanding Japanese civilization, and by sheer technological force penetrated the very orders that sent the Japanese navy into battle.

Mysterious as the East may be, the Japanese had to reduce the subtleties of their language to dots and dashes to wage modern war—and that was the Americans' big chance. Since the East was obliged to encipher its mysteries in the transparent language of Morse, the West in the person of American code-cracking specialists could copy out the messages, break them down at leisure, and without even meeting the East read its thoughts without help from Freud, Jung, or even Ruth Benedict. As early as the 1922 Naval Disarmament conference at Washington, American experts began exploiting this discovery. Their know-how worked so well that when East met West, West had already read the instructions radioed overnight from Tokyo to East's negotiators. Disclosure of these tricks in 1931 in a sensational book called *The American Black Chamber* did not prevent American black-chamber skills from mastering Japan's diplomatic code once again a decade later, enabling Roosevelt and Hull to know each morning what the Japanese representatives would say to them that day in the last weeks of pre–Pearl Harbor talks.

It helps explain, however, why the attack when it came was a surprise. The situation made the Japanese navy extra-watchful of its communications. When Admiral Yamamoto sent six carriers and thirteen screening warships out of Etorofu on November 26, he imposed a radio blackout so complete that the Americans never had a clue that the ships would arrive off Oahu nine days later to destroy the U.S. fleet on the first Sunday of December 1941.

As it happened, however, this success was the Japanese navy's undoing—and not only because it stirred the Americans to fight back. In the next six months the Japanese fleet was able to conquer so much territory that, far from keeping radio silence, it became of necessity the most talkative navy on earth. To run an empire that extended over a third of the globe, the Japanese had to take to the airwaves as never before. At their distant bases, they soon found, radio gear was as necessary as bullets and rice. Just to keep in touch with their conquests the Japanese navy had to print two million codebooks and — what was worse — distribute them, from the Indian Ocean to the Aleutians.

In a cave at Corregidor, in a basement at Pearl Harbor, and in barred and bolted quarters in Washington, American know-how tuned in on this talk, recorded it, reconstituted Japan's coding machines, weighed, sifted, and endlessly analyzed it. The name of this know-how was radio intelligence, and it applied its electromagnetic engineering and computational skills to the flood of Japanese messages in three ways. One gang of technologists zeroed in on direction-finding. This was a way of locating Japanese radio transmitters. Since radio signals are heard best when the receiver points at the transmitter, they rigged aerials that could be swung around until they heard the intercepted signal at its loudest. They set up several direction-finders to take bearings on the signal from different places around the Pacific and report them to their central control station. At the center they drew lines on a chart. The point at which the lines intersected marked the location of the Japanese transmitter. In this way it was possible to fix the location of a ship at sea, such as a submarine or task force flagship, and by successive fixes even to track its course and speed.

These findings did not only help keep an eye on day-to-day location of Japanese warships. They also provided the raw stuff for another brand of technologists — the practitioners of traffic analysis. When combined with direction-finding, it can often suggest where and when a planned movement will take place, something American commanders urgently wanted to know during the months of rapid Japanese advance.

Exploiting these technologies of direction-finding and traffic analysis, American know-how moved closer and closer to the jackpot of the radio intelligence game — namely, reading the messages themselves. Gradually the experts began to pry open the Imperial Navy's most secret cryptosystem, the two-part su-perenciphered D code. At best it was slow going, and crucial to all the arduously won gains was the fact that the Japanese were so busy trying to digest their conquests that they kept putting off the periodic changes of code that elementary communications security called for. As months passed and the Japanese still made no changes in the code, the Americans cracked call signs, learned to identify the originator and addressees of many dispatches as well as their time of origin, and then to recognize certain stereotypes in the text of the encrypted message itself. Noting such features and the length of the various dispatches,

When not at the stand-up intelligence desk in Flag Plot, the author worked in his quarters on photo interpretation duties—primarily, keeping custody of the huge quantities of reconnaissance photographs received.

developing a sense of "feel" by day-in, day-out scanning of the message flow, they learned to pick out the important ones. On these they concentrated, penciling and repenciling, conjecturing, sometimes turning for their most important clues to the translators, who were half cryptoanalysts themselves. Finally, as the Japanese found it simply too burdensome to change their code, and the scheduled date of code change was put off from April 1 to May 1 and then past June 1, the codebusters hit the jackpot. They penetrated the most important Japanese naval command dispatches. Intercepts carried from the Pearl Harbor basement to Pacific fleet headquarters gave Admiral Nimitz the information that enabled him in 1942 to place his few aircraft carriers at the right time and the right position in such widely separated places as the Coral Sea and Midway in May and June, and to surprise and defeat superior Japanese forces.

For those on the defensive, such intelligence of the attacking enemy is of paramount importance. After Midway, we took the offensive and it was we, not the enemy, who made and executed the plans that determined the course of the war. Intelligence of the enemy was therefore less central to our warfare. This did not much diminish the role of air combat intelligence: our information-expediting function proved to be such an active part of day-to-day air fighting that our efforts seemed almost more of an adjunct to naval air operations than a part of the intelligence branch dedicated to keeping track of the enemy and its intentions.

Of course eavesdropping on the Japanese still often paid off. The American technologists smashed their way into lesser Japanese communications even as the fleet code now eluded them. Aviation codes were probably the easiest to penetrate—for both sides. For the Americans from this time on, probably the most significant intercept intelligence was obtained from cracking the Japanese merchant-shipping code. Listening to Japanese convoy commanders announce their assembly points, their times of departure, and their estimated noon positions for days ahead, the basement technologists turned out information that enabled American submarines to succeed where the more highly touted German U-boats fell short. By dint of radio intelligence, they ambushed and sank so many merchant ships—110 tankers alone—that the Japanese eventually lost their capacity to wage war.

In the long and bruising Solomons campaign, the eavesdroppers in Hawaii sometimes got wind of plane movements in time for commanders to take defensive or even offensive action. Thus, after an eerie lull following the Japanese pullout from Guadalcanal in early 1943, intercepts enabled Admiral Nimitz to warn Halsey that the Japanese at Rabaul planned the war's heaviest raid on Guadalcanal on April 7. The tip, passed by Halsey to Gen. Nathan Twining, air chief in the Solomons, was the first word that the Japanese were back striking at Guadalcanal in force. There was just time to get the ships under way and fly all but fighter planes to the safety of Espiritu Santo.

Sure enough, early that morning a coastwatcher on Bougainville radioed, "Large flight of planes passing over. Headed south." Soon after other coastwatchers on Kolombangara and New Georgia reported more than 100 bombers passing overhead with fighter escort. That meant the attackers had not stopped to refuel on the way. Next, radar at Lunga Point picked up a huge bogey closing from 90 miles out. The American fighters stationed over the Russel Islands to the north spotted the Japanese formation.

At Fighter Two strip my ACI colleague John Marshall could see the planes falling. "We hoped they were not ours," he said. No fewer than 224 bombers attacked, 67 of them dive-bombers. Their own records show they lost 21 planes. Lt. Jim Swett's Wildcat burst through a cloud into their midst. He shot down three Japanese bombers as they dove, four more as they pulled out of their dives over Florida Island. Firing on the seventh he ran out of ammunition. His last shot killed the rear gunner, who slumped over his gun as Swett watched the plane hit the water. ACI Officer Peter Lewis made it his business to check Swett's claims. He found the seventh plane just offshore and learned from natives that they had found the gunner dead and killed the pilot. For his feat, Swett got the Congressional Medal of Honor.

The sudden flurry at Rabaul (the April 7 strike was followed by three big ones against New Guinea) led to one of the spectacular intelligence coups of the war. In their Pearl Harbor basement the codebusters and traffic analysts figured there must be an important presence behind such furious activity. Sifting the messages their attention was caught by the unusually large number of addressees for one dispatch. They swarmed over it, working all night, one filling in holes, another solving half a dozen difficult geographical code-identifications. By dawn they knew Admiral Yamamoto himself was at Rabaul. But they knew much more than that. The dispatch they had broken turned out to be an announcement of an impending visit by the admiral to the front lines, complete with a timetable of his movements. The message stated that Admiral Yamamoto would leave Rabaul on April 18 at 6 A.M. in a medium bomber escorted by six fighters and would arrive at Kahili airfield on southern Bougainville at 0840. The trip was to visit wounded soldiers evacuated from Guadalcanal and to thank them for their sacrifices.

Nimitz radioed Halsey: "Good hunting." There was time to lay careful plans, and Yamamoto was known to be almost compulsively punctual. At 0834 on April 18—exactly a year after Halsey had launched the Army B-25s on the Doolittle Tokyo raid—eighteen Army P-38s from Halsey's command made their separate approaches across the water toward Bougainville at 2,000 feet. "Bogeys, 11 o'clock high," said 1st Lt. Doug Canning in a low voice. Capt. Thomas G. Lanphier Jr., designated to make the attack, looked up and counted eight planes. Two were bombers. There should have been only one. As Lanphier dropped his wing tanks, the Zeros hurtled in. The two Japanese bombers dived toward the jungle. Lanphier kicked his plane over on its back. He plunged down and loosed a long, steady burst. The Mitsubishi's right engine and wing flared up. Lanphier's wingman, Lt. Rex Barber, closed in on the other Mitsubishi. He opened fire, saw the bomber shudder. He continued raking the plane and the top of its tail section broke off as Barber hurtled by. Looking back he saw "debris rising from the jungle" where the first bomber crashed.

The second careened into the water. Adm. Matome Ugaki, Yamamoto's chief of staff, with left arm broken kicked his way ashore and lived to fight again at Leyte. But Japan's war leader was dead. Yamamoto's ashes were duly put in a small wooden box lined with papaya leaves and taken on the superbattleship *Musashi* to Japan, where a million mourned at his funeral.

To Halsey went the exultant message: "Pop goes the weasel. P-38s shot down two bombers escorted by Zeros flying in close formation. April 18 seems to be our day." When Halsey read the message next morning at his regular conference, Adm. Kelly Turner "whooped and applauded." Said Halsey, "Hold on, Kelly. What's so good about it? I'd hoped to lead that scoundrel up Pennsylvania Avenue in chains, with the rest of you kicking him where it would do the most good."

Radio intercepts never served Halsey so well again. When Third Fleet went to sea the admiral continued to receive daily ULTRA dispatches from Nimitz's basement eavesdroppers filled with invaluable if sketchy clues as to enemy moves. But it must be emphasized that never during the battle for Leyte was it possible to read the command messages of the Imperial Fleet. On the other hand, so overwhelmingly, so decisively had Halsey seized the initiative that it was his plans, his intentions, his actions, not the enemy's, that determined each successive confrontation. We were constantly attacking. The force we wielded was air power—sudden, swift, and mobile as never before. We were moving fast, changing targets as each strike kept opening new opportunities.

In these circumstances, the critical intelligence was air intelligence: What were tomorrow's targets? What were today's missions? Above all, what was the outcome? Admiral Halsey and his commanders needed this kind of near-instant information that air combat intelligence could provide. So it was this kind of tactical intelligence we concentrated on — to such a degree that for us the line between operations and intelligence tended to blur. To the neglect of classical intelligence, of careful study of the enemy and his intentions.

By this time vast quantities of other kinds of information — terrain and beach studies, high-altitude photographs, crash intelligence (analysis of crashed enemy planes), prisoner interrogations, captured documents and so on — flowed in to Third Fleet's flagship. And as it happened in the crux of battle, here the most important intelligence of the seafight for Leyte would be found. And it was none of us ACIs but my roommate Harris Cox, the fleet intelligence officer, who seized upon a captured document sent over to us from the Southwest Pacific command and grasped that it held the key to understanding what the enemy was up to in the battle for Leyte.

And it's that story, transcending the limits of intelligence, that I'm going to tell.

3

PROTEAN PRELIMINARIES

DAWN, AND ADMIRAL HALSEY IS UP FOR THE DAY'S FIRST
flight operations, his fast carriers' strike in the central Philippines.

He moves quickly. His khaki shirt is open at the collar, with
wings pinned in place above the left breast pocket. His khaki
trousers are pulled tight by a web belt on which is attached a
spectacles case. His silver hair, close trimmed around large ears,
is only partly combed. His eyebrows, more black than gray,
seem to jut ahead of him as he strides onto the *New Jersey's* flag
bridge. Although he's not a big man, he has a head so big and
shoulders so wide that he seems almost to lurch as he walks. He
advances like a boxer, rising on the soles of his feet. There have
been times, tired hours in the South Pacific, when his step may
have been thought trudging. This morning he strides with a
spring. At 62, he is like a man going to a tryst.

A steel stairway has been cut through the battleship deck for
quick access to Halsey's Flag Plot command post. Out on the
deck he sniffs the air and draws a deep breath. He turns his
head in the wind. He hears the rush of water. He feels the sun,
already bright in these tropical waters. He always likes to take a
first look at the weather. When he took up flying in midcareer,
he likes to say, he had already chalked up more years aboard
destroyers than any man then active. He still has a destroyerman's nose for salt air.

His eyes take in his fleet—warships as far as he can see, smaller gray ones on the horizon, big gray ones sailing close by. On the big carrier tossing up a huge white bow wave scarcely a thousand yards away, Halsey can see the red-checkered flag flying high on the mast. "Fox is two-blocked," calls Signal Officer John Wilmerding, who turns and barks the same words through a tube to Flag Plot. The U.S. Navy's first assault on the Japanese in the western Pacific is under way.

IN FLAG PLOT, A DYNAMIC BUSTLE. AT LEAST TWENTY MEN were speaking into mikes, listening on headphones, bent over plotting tables. The senior duty officer, at his station before the big chart table, turned toward Halsey, trailing wires. He greeted the admiral and informed him that the carriers in company with the flagship—*Intrepid, Cabot, Bunker Hill*—were just launching deckload strikes. Radio relay planes were already heading for position to hear and transmit back to the fleet word from the first fighter sweeps over the day's targets.

Just to the left of the big operations chart table was the stand-up intelligence desk where we four intelligence officers took turns keeping air action reports up to the minute. Our chart showed how feebly the Japanese had fought back when Third Fleet's fast carriers attacked the southern Philippines three days ago: a thirty-two-ship convoy caught offshore and wiped out, docks and oil tanks a shambles at the port of Davao, and scores of planes caught on the ground and shot up by our attackers at six Mindanao airfields. Such weak opposition had led the admiral to shift to new targets in the central Philippines.

About these targets, about enemy forces in the area, we knew next to nothing—little more than what a network of Filipino guerrillas told us. No Allied plane had flown over the Philippines since MacArthur was lifted out of his Corregidor last-stand more than two and a half years ago. Our lectern chart showed only "important Japanese air strength" at Cebu, the day's main target, and "heavy naval and air concentrations" at

Manila from which reinforcements could easily be moved forward.

Air Group Two on *Hornet* had seen action first on shore at Guadalcanal, and only afterward on the carrier at sea. Most of its senior pilots had seen two tours of combat. The veterans of Fighting Two, led by Wild Bill Dean and known as "the Rippers" after downing thirty-three planes in an hour in the Marianas Turkey Shoot in June, had put in at Eniwetok. There they took aboard Ens. Cato Tillar, 20, of Emporia, Virginia, as a replacement pilot.

For weeks Tillar had been sitting on the beach with 200 other replacement pilots, subsisting on C and K rations in a flapping tent at the end of a runway, getting an occasional hop in an old crate to keep from totally forgetting what they'd been taught. The sun was so blazing hot that one noon Tillar's eyeballs rolled upward as he stood in the chowline. "I can't see," he shouted. Taken to sick bay he was treated for malaria and then sent away when that was not found to be the trouble. "Guess you had the blind staggers," the medic told him.

On *Hornet* Tillar found himself suddenly elevated to membership in the first team. What Churchill said of the Spitfire and Hurricane fliers in the Battle of Britain, that never was so much owed by so many to so few, might well have been said of the Navy's carrier pilots in the Pacific war. At the Coral Sea and Midway they turned the tide of war, handful that they were. And afterwards, never more than a thousand or so at any one time, they went on to inflict the Japanese navy's sharpest defeats. They were the warriors fighting a fight the likes of which would never be fought again, carrying the war to an enemy the rest of us hardly ever saw.

I knew a few carrier pilots in the islands, including some famous ones. There was for instance Gus Widhelm, who frequented our Bougainville tent when he was ashore starting up an early experimental night-fighter squadron. Gus had two Navy Crosses. Leading his SBD Dauntless dive bombers off

Enterprise and then *Hornet,* he was shot down twice. At Santa Cruz he surfaced in his rubber raft so close to the enemy force that he could tell us Japanese officers wore their whites even in battle. Later, as Admiral Mitscher's operations officer, he took it upon himself to land a plane on D-day morning on the Hollandia airfield. He claimed this was to see if it was suitable for use. Airmen have an adage: "There are old pilots and bold pilots but there are no old bold pilots." Admiral Mitscher benched his bold operations officer the moment he returned, but Gus had established that the Hollandia invasion was indeed a walkover. His successor by the time of the Philippine campaign was Jimmy Flatley, who, leading Fighting Ten, the fabled "Grim Reapers," had devised tactics by which the Navy's early Grumman F4F Wildcats could outfight the more maneuverable but also more combustible Japanese Zekes. Radio discipline was not always uppermost in Jimmy's mind. Young pilots especially liked to repeat the story how the insouciant Flatley, relinquishing a command on *Saratoga,* flew off radioing, "Goodbye to good old Sara—I mean Red Base."

Such oldsters, of course, had joined the Navy Air Corps before the war. Flatley, a boxer at the Naval Academy, had flown, always in fighters, with both Atlantic and Pacific fleets in the 1930s, and was already a seasoned commander when he won the Navy Cross shooting down six planes defending his carrier, the doomed *Lexington,* in the Battle of the Coral Sea. Those who manned the new fast carriers were young sprouts freshly and hastily schooled at Pensacola, Jacksonville, and Corpus Christi.

Hornet was the second big flattop to bear a name that went back to John Paul Jones's navy. The first flattop *Hornet* went down in the Battle of Santa Cruz. This *Hornet* was the fourth ship of fourteen of the so-called *Essex* class rushed to completion in World War II. This meant that the ship displaced 27,100 tons, measured 860 feet long (almost three football fields), and was powered by huge turbines that drove the ship at speeds up to 33 knots. The ship's complement numbered 3,500, most of whom were aboard to support the 700 or so airedales who were responsible for the big ship's striking power—at the time forty Grumman F6F Hellcat fighters, thirty-three Curtiss SB2C Helldiver dive bombers, and twenty Grumman TBF and Martin TBM Avenger torpedo planes—ninety-three planes in all. Rounding out the fast carrier strike force were the nine *Independence*-class light carriers (CVLs). Built on cruiser hulls, displacing only 11,000 tons, generating speeds up to 31.6 knots, they mounted thirty-five planes each—twenty-four F6F fighters and nine Avenger torpedo planes, no dive bombers.

Consider the wallop these new *Essex*-class carriers packed in their cavernous innards. Belowdecks, these seagoing airfields stored some 230,000 gallons of high-octane avgas—and air groups figured to use up 22,000 gallons per combat day. The ship's magazine held close to 1,500 bombs, ranging from 100-pounders to a dozen or so one-tonners that only Avengers launched into a stiff wind could carry aloft. These, and the thirty-six torpedoes stashed aboard, were constantly replenished from the support vessels that came forward with the oilers for mid-ocean refueling. Fresh stores and mail also came aboard at these meetings so that a carrier force could expect to operate 70 days at sea without having to return to base.

No question, these behemoths were vulnerable. Their sides were made of the thinnest armor plate: protective steel would have slowed them. Even their flight decks were made of wood (unlike the British carriers, all of which had armored flight decks). In the early days of the fighting, the Navy could muster no more than a thin screen of attending gunships; in the tide-turning year of 1942 the United States lost four of its seven carriers. After the task force's screening vessels grew in number and size, and the *Essex*-class carriers added some defensive power of their own, the United States lost only one fleet carrier—the light carrier *Princeton*—the rest of the war.

The new *Essex*-class carriers joining the fleet mounted twelve dual-mount five-inch guns, thirty-two 40mm automatic weapons in batteries of four, and some forty-six 20mm machine guns. In South and central Pacific experience, their gunners learned they could put up a good fight when attacked. And when they went up against the fortress islands along the Asian fringe, the fast carriers' guncrews showed they could not only fend off but shoot down shore-based aircraft that broke through screening defenses. In these confrontations, the five-inchers proved most effective firing at low-flying attackers. The automatic weaponry, the 40s drumming away like a railroad car with a flat wheel, and the augmented 20s firing at diving attacks from overhead, did well.

By the time Ensign Tillar reported aboard, Task Force 38 numbered eight *Essex*-class carriers — plus *Enterprise,* the "Big E" that had survived all the big fights since Pearl Harbor. It was hard to tell the *Essex*-class ships apart. They differed only in their camouflage coating. Every identifying mark had been painted out except the carrier's number. *Hornet* was CV-12. The old *Saratoga,* with its tremendous superstructure, was the easiest to identify. But *Sara* had endless troubles, spent a lot of time back at the Bremerton navy yard, and took no part in Halsey's forays.

What gave the *Essex*-class carrier its distinguishing silhouette was the island looming on the port side amidships. This was the ship's command center. All air and ship moves were directed from the island. The captain, of course, was himself an airman, and since flying rather than conning big ships was his long suit, surface-ship sailors sometimes sniffed disparagingly at a carrier skipper's shiphandling skills. Maybe so, but seasoned air commanders like TG 38.3's Adm. Frederick Sherman, who had captained a carrier in some of the war's sternest engagements, prided themselves on their cagey moves, wheeling into the wind at just the right moment to launch and recover planes, dodging under rain squalls when attackers closed, swinging their ponder-

ous vessels deftly to evade bombers plunging down from overhead.

The only carrier I ever spent time on was the second *Yorktown* (the first was lost at Midway)—and that was not for long.
Yorktown happened to be a flagship, so it carried eight ACI officers—one for the ship, one for the air group, one each for
the group's three squadrons, and two for the admiral's staff, plus
me on TAD—temporary additional duty. Nothing but an ob-
server. The ship's ACI office was in the island, just a few steps
from Flag Plot.

These great ships were America's capital ships from start to
finish of World War II. They were unique. They carried everything they needed to fulfill their sole purpose, which was to attack. The flexibility of their striking power—hurling rocket-
armed fighters, bomb-lugging dive bombers, torpedo-carrying
glide bombers—in assaults hundreds of miles beyond the range
of the Navy's biggest guns, was unmatched. Mobility was their
name, mobility and speed. Equally gratifying to the commanders who sent them on their marauding campaigns, they had a
capacity for sustained readiness that empowered them not only
to strike massively and suddenly, but also to keep attacking.

When they struck, air operations aboard couldn't wait for
dawn. The airmen were called first. On *Essex*-class carriers,
where each squadron had its own ready room in the gallery deck
immediately under the flight deck, pilots took their appointed
places. Togged in their heavy flying suits, they lounged uneasily,
each in his own big leather chair. And the ACIs gave them their
last-minute briefing, mostly via teletype strips on the panel
in the front of the room. "Pilots man your planes," came the
loudspeaker shout. A scramble, and the ready room went suddenly quiet. (Later, when kamikaze attacks kept penetrating the
wooden flight decks and spreading havoc in the gallery decks,
pilots suited up in wardrooms below and had to climb ladder
after ladder in their heavy flight gear to man their planes.)

GENERAL QUARTERS! A GONG RINGS IN THE MIDDLE OF the night, a bugle blows, and the bos'ns mate on watch wails, "GQ, GQ, GQ. Man your battle stations." And you do, fast. If you're my old tentmate Joe Bryan on *Yorktown,* you've placed your drawers inside your pants so that you can get into them in one leap. Might even have jammed your shirt inside your windbreaker beforehand so that you can throw them on as you exit down the corridor. Because two minutes after the bugle blows, every hatch and scuttle is bolted down, every door dogged tight. That's to keep fire, flooding, and other damage confined to the smallest possible space. This is known as Materiel Condition Affirm, and once it's set you can't get from one deck to another, can't even get through into the next compartment. So men rush down passageways and up ladders, buttoning their trousers, rubbing their eyes. Along the way are damage-control parties, posted to handle firehoses, shut off valves, and plug busted pipes—and see all doors dogged.

Topside, from your duty station up in the island, it's still so dark that the planes spotted on the flight deck are at first dim blurs. Gradually they solidify—Grumman F6Fs, our fleet fighters. The pilots are in their planes—actually not their "own" plane: it's a Navy singularity that each gets whatever machine is wheeled out for him. The assistant air officer takes up his bullhorn and his words come out as a bellow: "Prepare to start your engines. Stand clear of the engines." Fair warning. Watch out, easy to lose footing on the wooden deck and get hit by a spinning propeller.

"Start engines." The starter cartridges hiss and fizz but only three engines explode into power—a wet morning. So the crewmen have to wind them up, laboriously tugging the heavy propellers around to build up compression in the cylinders. One after another, engines come to life, until all are coughing and backfiring except the plane on the port catapult and the one behind it. They stay dead, and plane handlers shove them onto the No. 1 elevator (the ship has three) and send the planes down to the hangar deck below. The gaps they left are already filled before the elevator comes back up.

Now the roar of the engines shakes the ship. Pale blue flames flicker from their exhausts, reflected from the wet decks, and, even as you watch, the propellers blast the puddles dry. Taxi crew brandish red and green flashlights as they guide the planes into takeoff position. After the catapults explode the first few into the air, there's space for the rest of the deckload strike to launch in rolling takeoffs against the stiff wind created by the speeding ship. Yet danger remains present. Tolerances on a live flight deck are always small, and in a deckload strike they're minimal.

In a rush the planes are gone, and in Air Plot staff officers hear their radio chatter as they form up overhead for the day's mission. Much later they return. And that's when the other end of the vast flight deck springs into action. Across the after part of the flight deck stretch a series of steel cables that lift mechanically as each incoming plane makes its approach. These are the arresting gear, supposed to catch the tailhook dropped from the plane's tail and yank it to an abrupt stop. (There's also a wire screen amidships to keep an errant plane from crashing into planes parked chockablock with wings folded on the forward stretch of flight deck.)

But first the incoming pilots must obey the man standing on the little raised platform on the starboard edge of the ship's afterdeck. The landing signal officer, always a vastly experienced airman, calls the shots. Waggling paddles in each outstretched hand, he signals to the pilot the moves he must make to come in at just the right height and with wings level. If the pilot's approach is off center or too high, the LSO gives him a waveoff— and he must gun his engine and go around once more in the landing circle.

If his approach is okay the LSO gives him a cut—a swift slash of the righthand paddle across his chest. The pilot cuts his engine, the plane catches one of the restraining wires, and the plane pitches to a dead stop. Out dart the crewmen to unhook him, and either push his plane to the front of the flight deck or onto the elevator to be struck below to the hangar deck.

LANDINGS COULD BE HAIRY, ESPECIALLY AS BULLET-HOLED planes limped back with little or no gas left. Plenty of pilots cracked up coming aboard—and if bogeys were closing, the wrecked plane was simply shoved over the side. Of three replacement aircraft flown aboard *Yorktown* one day, one fighter came down so hard it blew both tires, an SB2C bounced 30 feet, then upended, its prop bent at right angles, and another F6, last in the landing circle, made ten passes before the LSO gave him a cut. No carrier ever landed planes after dark until the night after Pearl Harbor. Then Halsey's torpedo planes, returning from their vain search for the attackers, simply had to—and from that hour night landings happened all the time.

Someone said that operations on a carrier's flight deck was a scene of controlled madness. Hundreds of men darted about. Planes roared in, and men in red T-shirts swarmed around them. Planes had to be spotted quickly, and men in green jerseys ran about signaling them into position. Wild stories were told—like the harrowing tale of the lost pilot from another carrier who missed the flight deck, crashed on the carrier's port catwalk, and wiped out a ten-man guncrew. Or photographer Fenno Jacobs's story of how a returning Dauntless exploded as it landed, sending hunks of metal flying that wounded almost everybody top-side. But not Fenno, who chanced at that moment to be reaching down behind the waist-high metal parapet to pick up a roll of film he'd dropped. Such were the stories told. Yet at the same time *Yorktown*'s bakeshop was sticking candles on a mammoth cake to celebrate the carrier's 21,000th landing.

Just as big as the flight deck was the yawning hangar deck immediately below—really the ship's main deck, but given over entirely to keeping the ship's ninety-four warplanes flying. Eyebolts were everywhere on the huge floor, with mechanics forever tethering planes to them. Then the men swarmed over the crates, loading ammo, bombs, torpedoes, gasoline into them. This was where the deck crew performed overhaul and repair work. That SB2C with the bent prop—no problem, it was fitted out with a new one in a jiffy.

Belowdecks a flattop like *Hornet* was the equivalent of a fair-sized city. Certainly the mighty turbines that drove the ship could have lit a city the size of Toledo. And incidentally, the powerplant had been redesigned in these *Essex*-class carriers with alternating turbines and boilers. That way a torpedo that holed the ship underwater need not cause the ship to lose power all at once and force it to fall out of formation. All living quarters were below—wardroom and messing spaces, sleeping quarters, sick bay (a small hospital), bakery, tailor shop, chaplain's office, an elaborate radio layout, and a combat information center (CIC).

That CIC was a far cry from the old coconut-log command bunkers in New Guinea and the Solomons where the lights hardly worked, where orders to scramble more planes went out by the same bush telephone used by infantry platoons, and where on Munda I witnessed the next day's strike schedule being relayed by voice radio — through ear-splitting static — in Choctaw. These new shipboard CICs — and by late 1944 even surface ships down to destroyers installed them — had everything. They were the beginning of electronics. There, down in the bowels of the carrier, stood the fighter director officer (FDO), phones on his head, mike before his mouth, surrounded by men bending over formidable-looking machines.

THE CARRIER IS EVER ON THE QUI VIVE—AND AS NEVER before the CIC has become a primary battle control station. At this vital center the FDO scans his radar scope and gives orders to the task group's CAP. Eight or twelve F6s, these are the first planes launched, sent off even before strike planes at dawn's early light to begin an all-day CAP on guard high overhead.

Every few hours the formation swings into the wind to launch eight fresh F6s and recover the others. This goes on all day until dusk, the hour of maximum danger when more fighters are scrambled to beef up the CAP.

Aboard *Franklin* FDO Jim Winston gives orders to the pilots over voice radio. Before him is his upright plexiglas PPI — plan position indicator — panel, on which all the blips are displayed. Our planes are supposed to emit an electronic IFF signal that enables the FDO to evaluate the blips. He identifies the bogeys. And when bogeys close, he signals their course, speed, and "angels" (altitude) to the CAP pilots in time for them to make interception before the enemy reaches our ships.

Off Formosa or the Philippines, anything can happen. At the fighter director's side before the PPI panel stands his talker, grease pencil in hand. The talker drones: "Raid Two, bearing 237, 42 miles, closing . . . 239, 40 . . . 240, 37 . . . Raid Three, 221, 51 miles . . . Raid Two, orbiting . . . Raid Four 220, 43 . . . Raid Two opening. . . ." He plots every new position on the plexiglas dial, making a little *X* with a grease pencil, jotting down the time, and joining the *X*s to show the course.

Meanwhile, all the air frequencies being monitored by the CIC that should be silent are filled with the confusing chatter of pilots talking to each other. Too much talk, too much jabber, that's the bane of carrier communications. And through it all Winston has to evaluate these blips and get them right, fast.

Tension in the room is hardest on officers and men who have nothing to do, simply standing by, waiting to be called on. The CIC talker drones on: "Raid Five bearing 248, 51 miles . . . Raid Four 266, 34, closing . . . Raid Five 244, 47, . . . 244, 43 . . . 243, 38. . . ." The FDO speaks into his mike, and Capstan Two — Capstan is *Yorktown* and that's our CAP high overhead — shouts "Wilco," and dives where the fighter director tells him to. "Tallyho," he yells as he sights the bogey; interception follows.

As the other attacks turn away or fade from the screen, there is relaxation in the CIC and in Flag Plot, where the admiral's men are listening and tracking the moves on their own PPI panel. The admiral orders a turn. The deck tilts as the big ship heels to port. Pencils roll across the chart table, message boards sway on their hooks. And several decks below sleeping sailors roll in their bunks. Then the giant ship and its twenty attending vessels, each keeping station by its own ship's radar, steady on the new course. The talker says *Enterprise* has opened fire. A bogey is diving on the formation from 260. Alert, alert. Then the talker says, "Bogey is an F4U." That's the Vought Corsair gullwing interceptor, newly introduced in the fleet.

In the guntubs, on the signal bridge, on the flight deck, the tension drops off. Over the loudspeaker the bos'ns mate rasps, Boston-accented, "Set Materiel Condition Affirm Modified." Time to break for coffee.

THE HOTSHOT *HORNET* SQUADRON THAT CATO TILLAR joined set what Admiral Nimitz called "an alltime naval record" by shooting down 264 Japanese planes. Both his cabinmates were aces. Now he got steak for breakfast, ice cream every day. In the ready room, the others talked of nothing but going home. Flight Surgeon Jack Matthews worried about combat fatigue, but the senior pilots would not hear of being grounded. Lt. W. T. Blair, though his back hurt so he had to be lifted into his plane each time he flew, insisted on flying. In the Philippines Blair downed his fifth plane and thereby became the tenth squadron member to qualify as an ace.

In this company Tillar took part in a sixty-four-Hellcat fighter sweep, then was sent aloft to fly wing on a senior pilot in combat air patrol the day Halsey struck Mindanao. It was a combat hop, but no enemy was sighted. On the morning of September 12, as Halsey heard the VHF shouts on the radio frequencies in Flag Plot, Tillar flew again. His mission was to fly high cover for bombers striking Cebu and Mactan airfields. The sky was practically cloudless as the formation swept high over the mountains of Leyte. Tillar was flying wing on Lt. (jg) Tom Spitler. His logbook tells what happened next:

> We came down from 17,000 feet over Mactan to strafe, ran into four Zekes. One got onto my tail but I got him off and shot him down five miles southwest of Mactan island. I recovered and met two Zekes firing from two o'clock filling my plane full of 20-mm and 7.7 shells. I shot at them as they went by and "smoked" one.
>
> My oil pressure dropped and I lost altitude. Charlie Herbert called me and told me to make a water landing. Twenty minutes later I landed in the sea about 600 yards from Apid island.

Apid was a little island just west of Leyte. Friendly fishermen took Tillar ashore in outriggers. The islanders presented him with a dozen eggs, bantam size, and bade him eat. One, an almost naked former lieutenant of the Philippine constabulary, could speak a little English.

"At 1500 some VF-2 Hellcats located me and brought a Curtiss (floatplane) from the *Wichita*." Just as the floatplane taxied toward the beach, a man in a pink sport shirt and good trousers arrived in an outrigger from another island. In pretty good English he said he represented the guerrilla forces. Tillar had time only to ask about the Japanese on Leyte.

"He told me there were no Japanese on Leyte. 'There are only about 15,000 on Cebu,' he said." The floatplane, piloted by Charlie Spinelli, bore Tillar back to the fleet. It was still daylight when the young carrier pilot climbed aboard the cruiser. In one day he had fought his first dogfight, splashed his first Zeke, been shot down—and spent six hours in supposedly enemy territory. He was at once put in the hands of the *Wichita*'s doctor. Word came from the bridge that the admiral wanted to see him. Pilot and doctor went topside where Rear Adm. C. Turner Joy, a tall man, stood waiting.

Tillar had never before met an admiral. Shaky and scared, he was slow to speak. Abruptly, Joy turned to Tillar's companion and said, "Doctor, can you make him speak?" The doctor could. He returned with a bottle of Old Overholt, filled a tumbler. "I was scared," recalls Tillar, now a hardware store owner in his native Emporia, "I drank it like water. After that I told the admiral everything he wanted to know." And while the exhausted ensign slept in the admiral's sea cabin, Joy flashed word to Halsey: a rescued pilot reported no Japanese on Leyte and few anywhere else in the central Philippines.

At our standup desk in Flag Plot it happened to be my turn to tot up the day's strike results. The Japanese had been caught off guard. Rows of neatly parked planes on the two fields on Cebu and Mactan had been hit and set afire. The bombers wreaked havoc on shipping at Cebu. In all, our pilots flew 1,200 missions that day. I wrote up these results, and passed them on to Chief of Staff Adm. Mick Carney for transmission to Nimitz and MacArthur.

What was my surprise when I saw the preamble Halsey had affixed to the action report. He had Turner Joy's report, he had Task Force 38 chief Adm. Marc Mitscher's appraisal that Leyte was "wide open." Both Mindanao in the southern and Leyte in the central Philippines were on MacArthur's schedule for invasion. But first Halsey was under orders to land troops on Palau September 15, and at the same time MacArthur's forces were to land on Morotai, an island northwest of New Guinea. Not until two months later, after having methodically secured these stepping stones, Halsey was to occupy Yap and Ulithi in the western Carolines, the latter as a forward anchorage for the fleet, and MacArthur was to move up to take Mindanao. And only two months after that was MacArthur to land on Leyte.

"What are we waiting for?" Halsey asked his war plans officer, Marine Gen. William Riley. "Can't we skip Yap?" And he turned our action report into one of the most important naval messages of the war. As edited by Halsey it now read:

> Downed carrier pilot rescued from Leyte informed by natives no Nips on Leyte Bohol Apit or small islands in the vicinity. Planes report no military installations except bare strip on Leyte and no fields on Samar. Natives estimate 15,000 troops on Cebu. New subject: Preliminary report incomplete first day central Philippines strike 50 airplanes shot down and over 150 destroyed on ground. Several cargo ships and many small vessels sunk. Enemy air Negros-Cebu evidently reinforced over night. Air slugging match now going on. No attacks on surface ships yet.

Thirty minutes later a follow-up radio message went out to Nimitz and MacArthur from Admiral Carney's hand. It recommended canceling the western Caroline landings (except Ulithi) and reassignment of troops therefor to MacArthur for immediate seizure of Leyte.

An information copy for Admiral King in Washington found its way to the Joint Chiefs meeting with President Roosevelt and Winston Churchill at the Quebec summit. Halsey's proposal was just what President Roosevelt, facing reelection in November, wanted to hear. Speed up the war, move up the return to the Philippines to October? The instant reply was *yes.* "Having the utmost confidence in General MacArthur, Admiral Nimitz and Admiral Halsey," Army Chief of Staff George Marshall wrote later, "it was not a difficult decision to make. Within 90 minutes after the signal had been received at Quebec, General MacArthur and Admiral Nimitz had received their instructions to execute the Leyte operation." Date for the Leyte landing, moved up from December: October 20. Thus was triggered, what none then expected, the greatest seafight of all time.

Halsey would have liked to skip Palau, too, but by that time that was out of the question. Forty thousand Marines and soldiers were already at sea, and two days later they began their landings on Peleliu and Angaur islands. On September 21 Halsey's fast carriers delivered the war's first strike on Manila, plastering Clark and Nichols fields, the former bastions of American air in the Far East, and spreading destruction on merchant ships in the harbor. Our losses were 15 planes.

After a rest stop at the new forward base in Ulithi, Halsey and his fleet of a hundred warships sped northward. Our mission was to soften up the Japanese for MacArthur's invasion. We began at the north, striking first at Okinawa at the very door of Japan.

After a high-speed run overnight, we arrived undetected 200 miles off Okinawa. The dawn air sparkled: a typhoon had swept so close ahead that Halsey had briefly considered running under its cover a further 500 miles to strike Kyushu itself. "We achieved total surprise," reported Halsey.

First a hundred Hellcat fighters dived on the airfields, shot down the few defenders that got into the air, and riddled with tracer bullets those drawn up on the tarmac. Then wave after wave of bombers, the first at 0640 and the last at 1330, struck the air and naval bases on Okinawa and the surrounding islands. We claimed 111 enemy planes destroyed. We lost 21 planes, many of them "operationally," as the carriers maneuvered to launch 1,396 flights in six hours. Our bombers smashed 16 ships, including a submarine tender, a dozen PT boats, four cargo ships, and uncounted numbers of small craft. Hangars and dockside cranes took a beating.

Hoping to fox the enemy, Halsey pulled back to refuel before striking the next target, and that afternoon 61 Hellcats from *Independence* and *Enterprise* flew 325 miles south to attack an airfield at Aparri on the north tip of the Philippines. We claimed 125 planes destroyed on the ground and lost seven, six of them when a returning fighter went out of control and crashed into parked bombers on *Independence*'s flight deck.

It was a good try but the Japanese were not fooled. At least

16 bogeys appeared on our screens as Formosa-based snoopers made contact; our fighter patrols shot down three. On we rushed toward Fortress Formosa. "They knew we were coming," wrote Mitscher, and he was right. Halsey himself said later, "I should have struck Formosa first."

Again our pilots attacked with tremendous élan, first 203 stubby blue Grummans sweeping low over the island's airfields, then four successive bomber waves attacking airfield installations, hangars, barracks, fuel tanks. On the first attack our pilots shot down at least 23, on the second perhaps 60 Japanese defenders rose to meet them, and on the third no planes left the ground to intercept our attack. American casualties were much higher than at Okinawa—45 planes. *Trigger* and *Silversides,* the lifeguard submarines stationed offshore, picked up seven pilots and five crewmen. Still, losses that first day were heavy—29 pilots, 21 crew.

The Japanese responded to our onslaught with a fierce counterattack. If carrier war thus far taught lessons, it was that aircraft carriers were glaringly vulnerable. Deadly as was their sting, they were themselves highly susceptible to getting stung. In the Marshalls and Marianas, where islands were small and airfields few, our attacking carriers might escape unscathed. But now, sailing into close range of the big islands fringing the Asian continent, the Japanese held all the advantages of shore-based airpower. Formosa alone, with its fifty highly developed airfields, was a task force of unsinkable carriers outnumbering even Halsey's huge fleet. These were not coral island airstrips, these were their squadrons' permanent bases, with runways, hangars, communications, machine shops, barracks to match ours at Panama or San Diego. Within range were yet more powerful bases—in Kyushu and Honshu beyond Okinawa to the north. And could anyone forget that when the British battleships *Prince of Wales* and *Repulse* had ventured north from Singapore in 1941, shore-based Japanese torpedo bombers had smashed and sunk them?

Halsey pressed a furious three-day assault to knock out enemy air strength on Formosa and deny it as a staging base toward the coming landing on Leyte. On October 12 our carriers flew 1,378 sorties against Formosa, on the thirteenth 947, and the fourteenth 146. We claimed 500 planes destroyed, some two-score freighters sunk, heavy damage to ammo dumps, hangars, barracks, industrial plants. Actually, as we learned later, the Japanese lost more than 600 planes—more than the Luftwaffe lost in the entire Battle of Britain. In those same three days, we lost 100 planes or about 10 percent of our shipboard strength. And the diminishing number of sorties tells something of the force of the shore-based counterattack.

This was the Battle of Formosa, a "knock-down, drag-out fight between carrier-based and shore-based air," as Halsey called it. Day by day our planes gained command of the air over Formosa and inflicted heavy damage in broad daylight. But when night fell, Japan's land-based planes, counterattacking at dusk, tried to wrest away our hard-won supremacy.

And our carriers, our vulnerable carriers, gained the victory—but it was a near thing.

As long as daylight permitted, shipboard fighter directors at their radars radioed direction and speed of every incoming bogey, and our fighters, vectored to their tallyhos, successfully defended our force.

But at sundown the fighter directors called in their planes, and Japanese planes that had been hovering at a distance commenced their first torpedo-carrying attacks. They flew just above the wavetops. Nearing the force, the lead planes dropped flares to illuminate their targets—our ships.

As it happened, our TG 38.2 was furthest to the north of the four Third Fleet formations and thus bore the brunt of the first assault. We knew at once what was in the making. The dusk torpedo-plane attack had been a Japanese specialty ever since the carefully coordinated strike that sank the two British dreadnoughts near Singapore. Those of us who had served in the Solomons could not forget what happened five minutes after sunset on November 30, 1942. At that moment a twin-engine land plane dropped a flare suddenly silhouetting an American cruiser off Runnel Island—and seconds later eighteen other twin-engine Bettys wheeled in from the east to put four fish into the *Chicago*, which blew up and sank.

Now we watched anxiously as the deadly raid closed, only this time to fail. Torpedo-lugging Bettys skimmed in past the winking red gun flashes from our screening destroyers. Then the planes themselves glowed suddenly red as our ships' tracers caught up with them in the darkness. Before our eyes they cartwheeled one after the other in flaming arcs and exploded spectacularly in black geysers of smoke and seawater. This attack was ill-coordinated: to our radarmen at their scopes it seemed a piecemeal, hit-and-run succession of small, ineffectual dashes rather than any kind of organized assault. Not one torpedo hit its target, not one ship in our force was damaged. Such was the first evening, the evening of October 12, as we in TG 38.2, oblivious to the scale of the Japanese onslaught, experienced it.

By midnight our group commander, Adm. Gerald Bogan, figured we had destroyed nine planes by ships' gunfire. Groups 38.3 and 38.4, some 30 miles to the south, reported splashing three more—a total of twelve shot down. And on board *New Jersey* we got our first tip from Admiral Nimitz's ULTRA source that something really big was afoot: the commander-in-chief of the Japanese fleet appeared to be present in Formosa and directing the counterattack. Something called the T-force— a Kyushu-based torpedo-plane outfit—had been ordered forward in strength, and reinforcements were flying in from Shanghai, Amoy, and Hainan to join the all-out assault.

Although the thousand pilots on our carriers got little sleep that night, Halsey had seen nothing to deter them in what the Japanese commander-in-chief had shown so far. In spite of the evidence that the enemy knew where his fleet was and in spite of the mounting counterattacks, Halsey made ready to strike

Formosa hard the following day. His directive from Nimitz of October 5 was to "inflict lasting damage on installations and port facilities in Formosa," and he intended to do so.

Next dawn we could see the snowy peaks of Formosa's eastern mountain range, so close inshore were our ships as the carriers launched 115 fighters. The high-flying Grummans swept all interceptors from the air even sooner than on the first day. Bombers struck hard at the naval command center at Shinchiku. At least three waves of Helldivers and Avengers plastered the big Okayama, Keito, and Takao bases to the south. Fifty planes flew on to attack shipping and installations in the offshore Pescadores islands where we suspected reinforcements from Japan might be assembling.

That day we lost twelve planes in combat. But there were so many airfields, said Mitscher, that his planes "found it impossible to destroy all aircraft and neutralize all air installations." TG 38.3 reported finding not four but fifteen airfields in their assigned target sector in the northwest part of the island. In Flag Plot my roommate Harris Cox cracked, "Just as well the Washington brass decided we'd better not bother taking this island."

In late morning Mitscher ordered no further strikes launched after 1400 because he didn't want carriers to be recovering strikes at dusk. He also ordered that instead of arming bombers for a fourth strike all planes be struck below to the hangar deck. Another evening counterattack was shaping up. We had been snooped all day—CAP over the four groups reported shooting down twenty-one planes. But with sunset at 1826 and evening twilight ending around 1940, we faced a span of 74 minutes during which the force would be especially vulnerable to Japanese attacks.

Mitscher's estimate of the situation was right on the button. Eight *Belleau Wood* fighters flew out on a 270-degree vector to meet the first approach. At 12,000 feet they spotted a dozen Bettys. A layer of fighters flew cover a thousand feet above. The eight Hellcats climbed to 20,000 feet and dived. They wiped out five Bettys, then shot down five of the escorting fighters. The formation broke and fled.

That was only the beginning. Other attack groups awaited the approach of dusk. Then, as they started their run, they dropped to wavetop level to escape radar detection and to make fighter interception difficult. Their target was Adm. John McCain's TG 38.1. First anybody knew of their approach was when a lookout on *Wichita* yelled, "Betty at two o'clock." Eight planes attacked out of the blackness. Guns on the screening ships roared; within seconds six of the intruders caught fire and plunged into the ocean. One crashed so close to *Wasp's* starboard bow that a small fire started from scorched paint on the carrier's bow. At 1835 one attacker succeeded in launching a torpedo that missed the carriers but struck the cruiser *Canberra*. An explosion blew a jagged hole below the armor belt, flooded engine rooms and the after fire rooms, sent flames mast high, and killed twenty-three men. This plane was shot down by *Canberra's* antiaircraft fire.

At 1827, one minute after sunset, an attack group guided by a flare-dropping pathfinder began an attack on Adm. Ralph Davison's TG 38.4. At that moment the day's last planes were landing on *Franklin*. A plane swung toward *Belleau Wood* as if to enter the landing circle, but seemed slow to make its turn to the left. Said Ens. Bob Coleman, boss of the fourteen men crouching in a gunmount on *Belleau Wood's* starboard side:

> He still did not turn. Those two wing lights grew brighter and brighter. I yelled hit the deck. Over the director shield I saw a red light and a green light below me and a spinning spread of propeller between. The plane crashed into the ship's blister below and about 10 feet forward of us. A burst of flame shot up and through holes at our feet. With a leap I landed on the flight deck and dashed for the other side.

Belleau Wood put out the fire in a hurry. By the eerie light of Japanese flares, damage-control men found a 10-foot hole just above the waterline neatly plugged with the engine of a Helldiver. The pilot was dead, along with his crewmen and three members of Coleman's guncrew.

Meanwhile ten more attackers bored in. *Enterprise's* CAP, still airborne after sundown, splashed four. More bombers closed in scattered pairs over a 40-minute period. Ships' guns knocked down five, and an *Enterprise* night fighter, with the help of AA guns, sent a sixth crashing into the sea. Even so, other attackers dodged over the guns of screening ships and managed to launch torpedoes at *Franklin.* One fish was headed for the ship's bow, and *Franklin* evaded by backing fullsteam astern. Another passed harmlessly under the carrier. One of the bombers, already afire, tried to crash "Big Ben," as *Franklin* was called. It was too late for the big ship to turn as the plane came flaming in from the port beam. The plane missed the carrier's island, skidded across the flight deck, and crashed violently into the sea on the opposite side. Lt. Albert J. Roper jumped from his port battery as the wing of the plane, zooming right at him, caught and ripped the seat of his pants. A fourth Betty dove at *Enterprise,* burst suddenly into flame and splashed midway between *San Jacinto* and *Belleau Wood,* whose gunners broke into loud cheers. At 1908 *San Jacinto* gunners sighted the night's last attacking Betty. They took the plane under fire, watched a fire flicker in its port engine, then saw the plane blaze like a torch and fall into the sea a half mile astern.

We had already heard Radio Tokyo claim many ships sunk the first night. Evidently Japanese airmen mistook these fiery pillars rising from the sea where their own planes crashed as death and destruction for the U.S. Navy. This time Radio Tokyo broadcast their claim of four more carriers and a cruiser sunk, two carriers set afire and a battleship probably sunk. In fact, they had knocked out a total of one American cruiser.

On board *New Jersey* Halsey made a bold decision: *Canberra* would be saved, taken in tow 1,300 miles back to Ulithi, and Task Force 38 planes would cover its retreat with a third day's strike at Fortress Formosa.

By now ULTRA radio intercepts passed on by Nimitz confirmed that the Japanese were pulling planes out of Honshu and Hokkaido, China and the Indies, to mount attacks against us. So Halsey ordered a dawn sweep by planes from three of his four carrier groups over Formosa fields from which *Canberra* could be attacked. The fourth group he directed to hit bases in northern Luzon that were even closer to the crippled cruiser's track of withdrawal.

That day we lost twenty-three planes over Formosa, plain evidence that Japanese resistance was stiffening. And the Japanese high command, who seemed to credit their pilots' reports of thirteen ships sunk, obviously expected to finish off Third Fleet before the day was over. From Nimitz came an extraordinary intercept: at 1216 Imperial General Headquarters originated an order to form a force of cruisers and destroyers and as soon as ready rush south into the waters east of Formosa to attack and destroy the "remnants" of the vanquished U.S. fleet.

On this third day Mitscher's attackers broke off their strikes even earlier, and the enemy for the first time launched attacks by day. Our pilots reported intercepting army as well as navy planes, as if the enemy was attacking with all they had. More than a hundred planes tried to break through, but Task Force 38's CAPs swooped and broke up their formations. At 1510 a few Japanese attackers succeeded in penetrating far enough to attack TG 38.3 carriers, but without success. A few minutes later others closed on TG 38.2. At 1523 an enemy plane dropped a 250-kilogram bomb that exploded close to *Hancock*'s starboard bow, causing slight damage. Like a hockey team changing lines on the fly, the carrier took occasion to land a few planes. As Lt. Al Pope was making his final approach, he saw a Japanese plane screaming down at the carrier, so he jammed throttle on full power, took a waveoff, and blasted it into flaming fragments.

Thereafter the carriers beat off another daylight assault. Still another big formation attacked at 1712, and about twenty-five Japanese got far enough to make bombing runs at TG 38.3. A single plane dropped a bomb near *Lexington*. But again there were no hits.

Then came the dusk attack. Fifty-two twin-engine torpedo bombers, Bettys of the type that sank our heavy cruisers in the Solomons, closed in the day's third attack wave. They found Admiral McCain's TG 38.1 cruising just north of the crippled *Canberra*. Within 10 minutes a Betty, flying through the fire of screening destroyers, broke clear and dropped a torpedo that at 1831 struck the heavy cruiser *Houston* between the engine rooms amidships. Once again damage-control parties rushed in but the ship lost way. Other attackers released torpedoes at the carriers *Wasp* and *San Jacinto* but missed. *Reno,* dodging a fish launched by a damaged enemy bomber, received superficial damage when a chunk of the exploding plane landed on the cruiser's port quarter.

The sum total of the all-out Japanese air assault was thus to cripple two American cruisers. And now Halsey made another bold decision. Sure that he could still meet his commitment to neutralize Japanese air in the Philippines before MacArthur's landing on the twentieth, he called forward the oceangoing tug *Pawnee* to take the torpedoed *Houston* in tow, and informed Adm. Laurence DuBose commanding escort ships that he was now responsible for shepherding *two* cruisers to safety. Not only that, he seized upon new radio intercepts relayed by Nimitz to organize yet another attack.

Evidently on the strength of a top Japanese commander's report, decoded in Hawaii, that his airmen had sunk eight American carriers on the twelfth and three to five more on the thirteenth, Tokyo headquarters was now ordering the surface force alerted earlier to head south and knock off the "remnants."

No man to miss such an opportunity, Halsey convened a meeting around his wardroom table of what Chief of Staff Carney called "the dirty tricks department." Present were Air Officer Doug Moulton and Operations Officer Wilson, soon joined by Communications Chief Ham Dow and John Lawrence, ACI officer. Quickly their plan took shape. The admiral was as resolved as ever to save the two cruisers. Admiral McCain's TG 38.1 would cover them, and the cruiser escort, already jocularly dubbed "Cripdiv," was now to be "Baitdiv." To add to the rather flinty fun, Admiral DuBose in *Wichita* was to fill the air with dummy messages conveying an air of desperation—and the bulk of Task Force 38 would lie off to the east awaiting the chance to pounce on the advancing Japanese warships.

While this trap was being laid, Admiral Davison's TG 38.4 hit the Manila airfields and was subjected to air attack. Of three diving bombers, our gunners shot down all three. But the bomb released by one of the planes struck a corner of the deck-edge elevator on *Franklin* and exploded, killing three men and wounding twelve. At 1400 a second wave of ninety planes was detected flying out from Luzon. CAP broke up the attack, shooting down nineteen planes, including one whose pilot, we later learned, was Rear Adm. Masafumi Arima, touted as the first Kamikaze. Acclaimed as the warrior who "lit the torch" by crashing an American carrier (Goebbels's German state radio duly reported it that way), this supposed suicider was in fact shot down along with the other attackers before reaching his target.

On the sixteenth Halsey was ready to spring his trap, and he was looking for big game. Nimitz's ULTRA tips had put him up to it, and Halsey never forgot CINCPAC's directive that "in case opportunity offers or can be created, such destruction becomes the primary task." Deckload strikes were lined up and at the ready aboard two of his fast carrier groups, and search planes fanned out to stalk an enemy force that he was estimating on the basis of scattered reports could include as many as three carriers. Instead, at 1425, a *Bunker Hill* searcher found the actual force sent south from Japan—two heavy cruisers, a light cruiser, and four destroyers. It took until 1605 to unravel the report, which was garbled in transmission. By then it was too late to launch a strike, the Japanese were alerted, and the enemy surface force turned and hightailed it back toward Japan.

Disappointment in Flag Plot was tempered by what Third Fleet had accomplished, carrying the war for the first time to the inner citadels of Japanese defense. Carriers had fought and defeated all that land-based air could throw at them, and enemy air strength on the eve of the Philippine invasion had been substantially weakened. The funky little Cripdiv, the two damaged cruisers wallowing behind their tugs at 4 knots, inched clear of enemy air attacks and would with any luck make it safely to Ulithi.

"All Third Fleet ships reported by Radio Tokyo as sunk have now been salvaged and are now retiring toward the enemy," crowed Halsey in one of the war's famous dispatches. And Nimitz passed along a message from President Roosevelt: "The country has followed with pride the magnificent sweep of your fleet into enemy waters."

Indeed Halsey's sixteen flattops had bested Formosa's fifty airfields. Japanese air losses had been terrific. But there was another way to look at the Formosa fight. Task Force 38 had lost 100 pilots, a tenth of its strength. Its air groups had been tested at the limits of their endurance. What began at Okinawa and the first days at Formosa with such élan had shaded off—from 1,396 sorties the first day to 492 by the fourth. Falling back to refuel and reform while still hurling punches across the Philippines, the fleet lost any chance to stop in at Ulithi for mail and beer at Choppy Kessing's "Last Resort."

Halsey had to deal with some tough personnel problems, like relieving a carrier captain, calling down an insubordinate task group commander, sending an entire carrier to the rear without replacement. That was his drastic solution for *Bunker Hill* when TG 38.2's Admiral Bogan reported "a sad picture" on the big carrier October 21:

> Fighting Squadron 8 is practically 100% suffering from combat fatigue. Of 44 fighter pilots including four recent replacements, 20 grounded on recommendation of two flight surgeons. . . . Know conditions stated exist. Strongly recommend complete detachment Group 8.

Halsey's decision left Bogan's group 38.2 with just one big carrier (and two light carriers) with consequences on October 24 when that group had to bear the brunt of throwing back the main Striking Force of the Japanese fleet.

Shortly afterward word came from TG 38.1's Admiral McCain that *Wasp's* Fighting Fourteen, in like state, needed relief. Halsey replied, "Negative." All this was, of course, utterly confidential, but he also issued an order that "responsible seniors instill and maintain a resolute spirit in overworked pilots when stakes are high." On *New Jersey* some of us could see how unhappy he was when next he heard that *Lexington* pilots were near the end of their tether. He was seen pacing the bridge nervously until he blurted out to no one in particular but just thinking out loud, "Damn it all, I know they're tired and need a rest. So do all the other carriers. I'd like to give it to them but I can't—the morale of the whole fleet would be gone." He was a tough old salt but he had a heart and it hurt him to deny the rest they deserved.

And so, as the invasion day neared, Third Fleet's fast carriers pressed their attack. By the time they finished their A-day strike on the Manila area, we estimated that the Japanese had fewer than a hundred planes left operational in the entire Philippines. But we didn't realize the desperate lengths to which the enemy was prepared to go to halt this invasion. Great was our surprise when within three days after MacArthur's landing the Japanese flew in so many warplanes from Formosa, Okinawa, and Japan that they were able to mount wave after wave of daylight attacks against us. And when these failed, they would resort to the ultimate in desperation—war by suicide.

4

THE SUBMARINES

ALTHOUGH WE WERE TO COVER AND SUPPORT MACARTHUR'S landing—and did so with fighter sweeps and bombing attacks on Luzon on the nineteenth and close support for the landings on A day—Halsey's orders also read, "In case of opportunity for destruction of major portion of enemy fleet offers or can be created, such destruction becomes the primary task."

Both MacArthur and his Navy man, Admiral Kinkaid, had estimated that the invasion would bring forth no major Japanese response. Aboard the flagship *New Jersey* we maintained a continuous plot of enemy forces and watched for any movement that might signify counteraction. Three days after the Leyte landing, some of us in Flag Plot were still wondering how the Japanese fleet might react—maybe not much at all.

Not so.

In the sea's vast darkness the submarines *Darter* and *Dace* were two minnows as they drew together. By voice radio Cdr. David McClintock, lean, young skipper of *Darter* and leader of the two-boat "wolfpack," had set up their midnight rendezvous. They were to plan the "remainder of coordinated patrol," he said, in the strategic waters between Borneo and the southwestern tip of the Philippines.

The two subs exchanged messages by line-throwing guns, and McClintock and his fellow-captain, black-eyed Bladen Claggett Jr., also Annapolis '36, went below to read over the communications in the dim red light of their submarine control rooms. On deck the lookouts shouted back and forth through megaphones.

Suddenly an urgent voice broke into the tropical night. At the scope in *Darter*'s conning tower radarman Ray Jones gave a shout: "Contact—maximum range—could be rain." McClintock leaped up from his table in the control room below and scrambled up the ladder to the conning tower. The blips he saw on the edge of Jones's screen were already unmistakable. This was no raincloud. The blips were big. And they were moving fast—too fast, Jones said, for merchantmen. Jumping out on deck, McClintock grabbed a megaphone from the officer of the deck and yelled across to *Dace*, "We have contact. Let's go." It was 0017 on the morning of October 23.

At that very moment *Dace*'s radar went out. Until Claggett's men got it working again 30 minutes later, they took their signals from *Darter*, and *Darter*'s skipper was in no doubt. "Heavy ships at 34,000 yards, advancing in two columns," McClintock told Claggett on voice radio. "Follow me."

The contact was at extremely long range, far beyond the usual 18,000-yard reach of submarine SJ radars in these waters. *Darter* was lucky. Their rendezvous had drawn the submarines seriously out of their assigned positions. It was nowhere near Balabac Strait, the channel between Borneo and the Philippines and the shortest route from the Singapore area to MacArthur's Leyte beachhead. It was also well to the west of Palawan Passage, the other strategic gateway they were supposed to guard. But the big ships on *Darter*'s screen had given Balabac Strait the go-by. They were heading north through Palawan Passage, between Palawan, westernmost of the Philippine islands, and the treacherous South China Sea shallows known as the Dangerous Ground. At this moment they were on a course at right angles to their bearing from the two submarines, which was another big stroke of luck for *Darter*. Not only had the submarine's radar picked up the Japanese force at extreme range, it had done so at the one moment where this was possible. For on their course of 060 true the Japanese ships would within moments have passed beyond the furthest sweep of *Darter*'s radar.

Such are the fortunes of war. Adm. Ralph Christie, chief of MacArthur's submarines, had stationed *Darter* and *Dace* at this important crossroads precisely to watch for any Japanese naval forces on the prowl. But like others in the Southwest Pacific from MacArthur on down, Christie didn't really think the Japanese fleet would come out to fight for Leyte. It was already the third day since the landing, moreover, and still there had been no sign of big ships. Earlier *Hammerhead,* posted further south between Singapore and Borneo, had seen nothing (*Hammerhead* had attacked a convoy and thereby missed their approach). Only that afternoon, obviously ready to ease up on the watch, Christie had given *Dace* permission to hunt a merchant convoy reported by a plane to the north. That was why the two submarines had pulled north and west from their lookout station.

And now, having made contact, *Darter*'s youthful skipper knew at once that he had caught wind of a major Japanese task force, and lost no time reporting it. As he raced off with *Dace* to attack, he broke radio silence even though that might set the enemy on guard against his approach. At 0230 he flashed the big news: a formation of Japanese warships was on the loose and headed on a course that could take them, via the Palawan Passage, to attack the American invaders at Leyte.

McClintock's first flash report, beamed to Admiral Christie in Australia and relayed to Halsey on *New Jersey* at 0620, was our first intimation that we might be in for a real fight. The whereabouts of the Japanese heavy ships, hitherto a mystery, was now known. This message, which arrived early on the twenty-third when I was on watch at the standup desk in Flag Plot, was one of the most significant contact reports of the Pacific war. This is how the message relayed by Radio Melbourne read:

SECRET. URGENT. 108-S FOX 4253 from Task Unit
71.1.4 [*Darter*] to CTF 71: *Darter*'s No. 6. Three probable
battleships 0100/H 23rd 08 28N 116.30E, c. 040, speed 18.
Radar pips 34,000 yards. Closing.

Submarines in the Pacific were a fleet apart—apart from the
ships in their task forces and the planes in their tight formations. They came and went silently at their bases on the far
coast of Australia and at the West Loch in Pearl Harbor. Not
that they were unknown to the rest of the Navy—three of
the four top commanders, including admirals King and Nimitz, were submariners who wore their dolphins as proudly as
aviators wore wings. Airmen were glad for the submarines that
stood lifeguard off the distant targets and fished them out of
the water when they were hit and had to ditch at sea. The fleet
relied on their early scouting messengers to alert the forces of
enemy ship movements. And in a less informed way the other
branches of the fighting Navy knew that the submariners were
going out on patrols far beyond everybody else's limit—off
to the China coast, to Singapore, to the Empire itself—and
steadily sinking merchant shipping on which the Japanese depended for oil and other supplies brought at great effort from
the Indies.

And yet the rest of the seagoing Navy could never know what
the submariners went through. Warships traveled in company,
airplanes flew wingtip to wingtip, but submarines voyaged alone
—not just for a day but often alone for two months' war patrol.
Submarines traveled so far that they sometimes spent most of
their time just getting to their assigned station. At their two
bases, one at Pearl Harbor, the other at Fremantle in western
Australia, they took on their twenty-four torpedoes and 80,000
gallons of diesel oil and went out on their war patrols. Usually
but not always (the U.S. Navy lost 52 of its 288 submarines in
the Pacific) they returned, sometimes with a broom tied to the
periscope signifying patrol waters swept clear, all torpedoes ex-

pended, many ships sunk. Two weeks ashore followed, and no
one who knew anything about the Pacific war begrudged Admiral Nimitz's decision to hand over Honolulu's grandest hotel,
the Royal Hawaiian, to the men for their between-patrol shore
leaves. The submariners, 85 percent of them reconverted civil-
ians, consumed quantities of beer and bourbon. Then, with a
little help from the Shore Patrol, they reassembled at the dock in
Pearl Harbor. They went aboard their boat and took it out to
sea for a day's tuneup drill—I once went out in *Haddock* for
this no-nonsense refresher—with a destroyer. Then back to
Pearl and next morning, loaded with a supply of 500 pounds of
coffee, 2,400 pounds of beef, and those twenty-four torpedoes—they took off in their submersible pullman 6,000 miles
to the Empire. This consigned them to six to eight weeks in
closest quarters, not to be sure living all that time without once
surfacing as some nuclear subs could and did during the Cold
War years. But these boats were only 300 feet long, and in the
war zone they generally operated submerged all day and only
surfaced at night. Even then few crew members had duties that
brought them into the open air. You had to be a certain kind of
person to survive a war patrol; not everybody could do it, and
aviators in particular snorted that they could not understand
how anybody did.

On a submarine, far more than on other ships, everyone had
to work and live as a team. When the boat dived, the lives of all
eighty on board depended on each man performing his individually assigned task. Even the cook had to secure the galley
sink. At that moment every man stood absolutely immobile,
speaking his part, reading gauges and meters and repeating the
readings, repeating and giving orders, in muffled voices, like
whispers echoing in a deep well. The engineering officer had
already computed the weight of everything that came onto the
boat—every grapefruit and all the fuel and each man. But at
each dive he had to calculate exactly how much seawater must

be let into the ballast tanks so that when the boat went down it would weigh exactly the same as the water it displaced. Everybody peered at the "Christmas-tree" panel, watching for each light to wink green. Each reading had to be right, each time the boat had to trim, or else it might not surface again.

Underwater mutuality there had to be, more than enough to close tight ranks in Saturday-night street fights in Pearl City. One war patrol wove the same ties that helped an infantry patrol survive on nightly jungle patrols in Guadalcanal or Vietnam. But for submarines there was more buddy business than most could stand. Aboard their pigboat, crewmen simply had to get along. There was no way of avoiding each other. Amid annihilating propinquity it was absurd to seek privacy—but they did. A lieutenant on *Shark,* unable to stand the eating habits of a fellow officer, might contrive his watch-standing turns to take his meals in the boat's tiny wardroom without once in a whole year eating in the other's company. If Communications Officer Bob Brady of *Besugo* had to walk through the crew's mess, where thirty-two bunked, on his way to the forward torpedo storage, he tried not to see anybody. "Look, Mr. Brady," said *Besugo*'s chief of boats, "a man's sleeping in the crew's mess — 64 stinking feet, 64 armpits, breath and other gases everywhere, bodies 18 inches apart—what does he want with you?" Quartered with the sub's six other officers, the lowliest ensign lived better. The mildest thing said in the crew's mess was "Officers never listen to enlisted men." Once Brady manned *Besugo*'s sound gear alongside a veteran chief overdue for stateside reassignment. Overhead a Japanese destroyer "pinged" so accurately at the cornered quarry that its echo-ranging signals bounced back to the submarine's listening gear. Brady, pale and perspiring, was thus enabled to call out to the captain the destroyer's distance as it drew closer: "800 feet—725—600." At that moment, when all waited helplessly for the depth charges to drop on their heads, the ship unaccountably turned and went away. Brady looked at the chief, unbelieving. The chief looked back and said, "See, the fucking *Japanese* officers don't listen to their enlisted men."

At any moment of importance the captain conned the ship. He was a young officer whose rank was invariably below that of captain. On occasion his number 2—the exec—took over. The circumstance of supreme importance was the attack. Then the submarine became a gun, a double-ended six-shooter that could fire torpedoes from six tubes in the bow or six others from tubes pointing back out the stern. Any one of these deadly fish, running 30 to 35 MPH, could plant 860 pounds of steel-wrapped high explosive against the hull of a target ship up to 7,000 yards away.

When it was time to shoot, the captain took the all-important post in the conning tower. There he fixed his eye on the periscope glass, which he raised and trained by grasping and turning the two handles. At that moment the submarine had only this one eye, this one pair of hands. The captain stalked the target. The captain brought the target before the single eye. Only the captain trained the boat's sight upon it. Only the captain decided when to shoot. Only the captain gave the command to fire torpedoes. Only the captain saw them run. Really, the submarine with its eighty men was nothing but the obedient servant of this one man.

On the eve of the Leyte battle the United States had forty-four such eyes tracking the waters between Hawaii and Asia; at that moment the Japanese had eighteen operational submarines at sea. All were roughly the same size, that is to say, much larger than the German U-boats and other submarines developed to work in the narrower seas off western Europe. For decades the Japanese had made much of the role of submarines in attacking the enemy fleet, sinking big ships, and making it easier for the surface force to finish off the weakened foe. They called their submarine fleet the Advanced Expeditionary Force and in the war's first years scored a number of successes against major U.S.

ships. The I-7 sank the carrier *Yorktown* at Midway and the carrier *Wasp* down in the Eastern Solomons, and Japanese boats twice torpedoed the carrier *Saratoga* when the United States could ill spare a single carrier. But by 1944 more than half the Japanese boats had to be used to run supplies to bypassed island bases. And as the United States brought to the Pacific the escort carrier, the hunter-killer group, and other weapons developed to defeat the Germans in the Atlantic, Japanese submarines lost their capacity to sink ships. Although, as we later learned, ten submarines were sent to attack our fast carriers and invasion convoys east of the Philippines in October, the sum total of their offensive action was the torpedoing and sinking by I-19 on October 25 of the Seventh Fleet destroyer *Leutze* off Samar.

As Halsey saw it, the boats could operate as a kind of picket line to alert him to any Japanese move to intercept his attacking fast carriers. In the Southwest Pacific area, submarines like *Darter* and *Dace* were under MacArthur's control. But most boats patrolling the Pacific got their orders from Adm. Charles Lockwood, Commander Submarines, Pacific Fleet. Lockwood's headquarters were only a few hundred feet from Admiral Nimitz's. Before setting off to raid Okinawa and Formosa, Halsey demanded that submarines operating in that area be placed under his control. With an eye to intercepting any Japanese naval moves against him, Halsey sent Nimitz a plan for stationing one boat every 50 miles or so between Okinawa and the China coast.

Nimitz turned him down. His standing orders gave the submarine command two missions, of which "the interception, reporting and destruction" of Japanese fleet forces was only one. The other was "the destruction of merchant shipping." When he sent Halsey a lineup of thirty submarines that could "give you the closest possible support," Halsey replied, "The dispositions appear to have gaps." But the arrangement worked well enough during the big air battle off Formosa in early October. On October 14 *Besugo,* leader of the three-boat wolfpack Lockwood had stationed in Bungo channel south of Japan's Inland Sea, was right on the job at the right time. The submarine's skipper, Cdr. Tom Wogan, sighted and correctly reported the force of cruisers and destroyers moving south from the Inland Sea to pounce on what the Japanese thought were Halsey's "remnants." With *Besugo*'s help Halsey was able to lay an ambush for the Japanese instead.

But the urge to go after fat merchant-ship targets was strong among submariners, and neither Lockwood nor Christie dared tell their skippers beforehand that MacArthur was going to invade Leyte on October 20. For five days after spotting the Second Striking Force's sortie, *Besugo*'s wolfpack kept watch in Bungo channel, battling heavy swells and watching their fuel dwindle without so much as one shot at a target. Finally, on the evening of the eighteenth Wogan signaled Lockwood: "Consider primary mission of this group is now to attack." Without demur from Lockwood he pulled his boats off their lookout stations and went back to the everyday business of chasing convoys. To this end he moved *Besugo* and *Ronquil* to the west of Bungo to catch smaller ships hugging the Kyushu coast. The third boat, *Gavilan*, went off to patrol near Kii channel several hundred miles to the east.

That left the east side of Bungo uncovered. Five days after *Besugo* spotted the cruiser force leaving the Inland Sea by that route, the Japanese carrier force departed for Leyte, warily hugging the eastern shore. Their commander said later he thought he would have to fight his way through a ring of submarines. Instead he emerged into the Pacific completely undetected, all because Admiral Nimitz declined to order overriding priority for the offensive reconnaissance Halsey wanted in support of his fleet operations.

FULLY 24 HOURS BEFORE DARTER'S ELECTRIFYING REPORT Halsey had begun receiving ever stronger hints in *New Jersey*'s Flag Plot that the Japanese navy was not going to let Mac-

Arthur's October 20 invasion go unchallenged. At 0747 on the morning of October 22 Admiral Nimitz radioed his estimate, on the basis of radio intercepts, that the Japanese Mobile Fleet, or carrier force, had left the Inland Sea "recently, probably on October 20." No fewer than nine of our subs patrolled the waters west of Luzon Strait where chances of merchant-convoy targets were thought especially favorable, and they kept running into warships. *Seadragon* made a night attack on a force of seven warships and claimed two torpedo hits on one, which it identified as a carrier. Late on the evening of the twenty-second the submarine *Shark* sent word that earlier that day it had made contact with a force of seven warships headed on course 190 through waters south of the Pescadores islands at a speed of 22 knots. Looking at our intelligence chart in Flag Plot, Halsey could see that these might be reports of the same seven warships.

But now *Darter*'s messages, arriving one after another on our flagship, provided the first solid information suggesting that the Japanese navy was reacting after all to the Leyte landing. McClintock's second flash report announced the presence of at least nine ships and "many radars." A third report at 0445 enlarged the estimate again: "Minimum eleven ships. Same course, speed." Still running to get into attack position ahead of the Japanese force, McClintock knew only that it was a big one. Not until much later did he become aware that "we had before us the largest submarine target of all time."

Halsey sat down at his big wardroom table and looked at the dispatches Operations Officer Rollo Wilson handed him. Identification of ships—a submarine could go wrong on that, Mick Carney said, but not on course and speed. "He's trackin' 'em, and every one of his reports says they're headed straight up the channel and at 16 knots," said Wilson. "At that rate they could get to Coron Bay by sundown," said Doug Moulton.

Assistant Operations Officer Bill McMillan brought down another dispatch from Flag Plot. It was from *Icefish*—a contact at 0930 the day before on two heavy cruisers and three destroyers headed south through the waters where *Seadragon* and *Shark* had made their sightings. Rollo Wilson telephoned Ed Lile to plot the track of these ships if they should steer for Coron Bay. Lile called back a minute later to report that these ships could easily arrive at Coron Bay by sundown. Unclear their mission — but evidently major Japanese naval moves were under way.

What were they up to? Before MacArthur's invasion, Halsey had thought the Japanese might scatter their warships in small, dispersed groups within easy sailing distance of Leyte — and then concentrate them quickly for short, fast Tokyo Express runs. That possibility brought vivid memories of the South Pacific. In the Solomons the Tokyo Express was any group of Japanese warships, usually destroyers, that raced south to land troop reinforcements night after night on Guadalcanal. It was so named because, like a train, it ran on schedule. It was hard to derail.

Bill Riley reminded the others that in his Leyte plan MacArthur had mentioned a second possibility: the Japanese might carry out naval raids on his exposed transports. That turned everybody's thoughts to the night after the landing at Guadalcanal in 1942. Kelly Turner, the amphibious commander, pulled his transports out the first night. No one who had been in the South Pacific could forget that night, the night a force of Japanese cruisers caught our side flatfooted off Savo Island and sank four cruisers. But now, Carney pointed out, the Japanese force included battleships, at least four of them. Four was as many battlewagons as were now deployed in the two task groups Halsey had designated to defend the approaches to Leyte. Moulton, Halsey's air officer, spoke up. MacArthur's plan, he said, also specified a Japanese capability of making air attacks on his ships unloading at Leyte. Our four weeks of slashing attacks had won us air supremacy over the Philippines. But if the Japanese now tried a strong naval action, he said, you could expect them to try to fly in air reinforcements, maybe from China, maybe from Japan itself. In that case the 388 planes of Sherman's TG 38.3 and Bogan's TG 38.2 might not be enough to hold air command over Leyte.

While Halsey's staff debated on *New Jersey* 600 miles to the east, Kinkaid, MacArthur's naval commander, wrestled with the same question on his command ship in crowded Leyte Gulf: what were the Japanese up to? He, too, plotted the course of the Japanese heavy ships advancing along the opposite side of the Philippines. To his mind, their destination was Coron Bay, where radio intercepts indicated tankers were gathering. After the Japanese got to Coron Bay, anything could happen. They were only a day's sail from the transports and landing craft for which he was responsible. He was glad he had ordered his replenishment group to enter the gulf rather than stay at sea to the east. That meant at least that his Seventh Fleet's big ships, the old battleships and cruisers he had brought along to screen his transports and shell the invasion beaches, would not have to leave the scene to refuel.

Kinkaid, like MacArthur, had planned the whole amphibious operation on the premise that the Japanese fleet would not come out to challenge a landing at Leyte. That was stated in both their attack plans. It was even stated in Admiral Mitscher's plan for Third Fleet's fast carriers. It was Nimitz's expectation as well: he had set the date of November 11 for the Third Fleet's attack on Japan, and at no time in directing Third Fleet to help MacArthur had Nimitz suggested by the slightest word that this schedule was not firm. You did not lay plans for an attack on Tokyo requiring every ship and plane of our fleet if you anticipated a major action with the Japanese fleet just beforehand.

As *Darter*'s reports rolled in, Kinkaid also studied the confusing sightings signaled from northwest of the Philippines. From scattered submarine reports of southbound Japanese warships he concluded that a force, probably cruisers and destroyers, was advancing to Coron Bay.

But he also noted that at least two aircraft carrier sightings had been reported in the South China Sea—not only *Sea-dragon*'s but another further north by a China-based plane of Gen. Claire Chennault's Fourteenth Air Force. Uncertain as these sightings might be, Kinkaid drew from them the conclusion that at least some carriers had arrived in these waters from Japan. On the morning of the twenty-third, therefore, he issued his revised estimate of what the Japanese were up to. At 1042 he radioed Halsey: "I regard the approach of enemy combatant ships and tankers toward Coron Bay as the first phase of the buildup of magnified Tokyo Express runs against Leyte. . . . It is also possible that enemy carriers will support surface forces and strike from west of Palawan." In short, Kinkaid saw the approach of the heavy ships as presaging some sort of move to land reinforcements at Leyte—either at Ormoc on the Japanese-held west side of the island, or possibly by a rush through Surigao Strait to some area where the Japanese still held on in eastern Leyte. Kinkaid also warned of "indications of a concentration of a large number of enemy aircraft in the Luzon area" in support of the "magnified Tokyo Express runs."

On board *New Jersey* Halsey, like Kinkaid, was re-estimating the situation. He was more than mindful that the fast carrier raid on Japan was his next big scheduled operation and would require every ship and plane Third Fleet could muster. He saw no reason to change his judgment that he had all but demolished Japan's land-based air strength in the Philippines. But he had also been reminded sharply by Nimitz on October 19 that the limitations set by the necessity of giving close cover to MacArthur remained in effect. Not only did Halsey seem to accept these limitations but the night before he had sent MacArthur congratulations on returning to the Philippines and said he hoped to "swing some blows in support" of MacArthur's efforts to expand the beachhead.

It was Admiral Carney's habit as chief of staff to sum up the situation and pose the choices for Halsey. This was fine with Admiral Bill. Mick was the smartest mind and quickest tongue on the ship, and Halsey said later, "I had sense enough to know that I had a man who could talk so well, and I used him as I am not in his class in that respect." Carney had conducted the negotiations with MacArthur and his staff when Halsey's island-hopping operations carried him further into MacArthur's Southwest Pacific domain. He spoke for the admiral on many other occasions. Now Carney said, "No operation plan can ever include the enemy's reactions. We must always be ready to make instant decisions on changes in the situation resulting from unpredictable enemy reactions."

With their big ships converging on the Philippines, said Carney, the Japanese had three possible courses of action. First, they could try to reinforce their ground troops on Leyte with fast Tokyo Express runs. That was what we first expected. They could still do it, said Halsey. But the approach of the heavy ships seemed to signal something more, Carney continued. The Japanese could mount air and surface raids on MacArthur's forces on the beach. They did that at Guadalcanal, said Halsey. Everybody remembered that infamous first night at Guadalcanal. But Halsey had later actions in mind—when months later they sent battleships close inshore to shell men and planes on the beach. Carney said there was a third possibility: the Japanese could make a major naval attack on the Leyte forces. Halsey said he had never seen them do that, even at Guadalcanal. Carney had a way of pushing his rimless glasses up on his balding forehead. Summing up he now scowled: Third Fleet dispositions needed beefing up.

As Carney spread the chart on the table, the tanker *Neosho* was coursing alongside *New Jersey* at 10 knots, pumping oil through its hoses into the flagship's tanks. On the *Neosho*'s other side, the cruiser *Miami* was also getting a drink. Off to starboard the big carrier *Hancock* was taking oil from the gray belly of *Ashtabula*. Two destroyers were alongside *Monongahela* filling their tanks. Admiral Bogan had reported that fueling for our task group was on schedule and would be completed by noon. Looking at the chart, Halsey saw that he could send TG 38.2 to join Sherman's TG 38.3 close inshore east of the Philippines—and still get both of these task groups back to their next fueling rendezvous 500 miles east of Leyte on October 26.

Carney resumed. We can see, he said, that the Japanese forces converging on the opposite side of the Philippines add up to at least eighteen ships, probably more. We know from radio intercepts that the Japanese have kept six battleships in the Singapore-Brunei area, and we now know that there are battleships among the heavy ships moving into the Philippines—at least four. And the two fast carrier groups now disposed in support of MacArthur have no more than four battlewagons—not good enough.

The air situation also had to be reconsidered. Of course, Carney said, we have to expect the Japanese to rush more planes into the Philippines if their big ships try some action. These would doubtless be planes operating from fields in the Philippines. But several carriers had been sighted, as Kinkaid pointed out, in the South China Sea. So attack by Japanese carrier planes from that direction could not be excluded, even though the 300-mile distance between Leyte and the waters west of Palawan would probably force such carrier planes to operate from shore bases, too. All things considered, said Carney, Third Fleet's air strength should be augmented, too, although that is probably not so urgent as adding to our gunships.

By this time Halsey had decided that his previous plans for his fast carrier forces would not do. In view of his instructions to support MacArthur, reemphasized only the day before by Nimitz, it was now imperative to clarify the enemy picture. Even if Kinkaid was right, and the enemy intended no more than "magnified Tokyo Express runs," Japanese battleships were now within a day's sail from MacArthur's beachhead. To be ready for either a troop run or a Savo Island–type raid Halsey would have to realign his forces and bring forward three rather than two of his fast carrier task groups. Accordingly, he said he would leave Sherman's TG 38.3 right where it was—just 90 miles east of Luzon. Second, he would change Bogan's orders. Instead of joining Sherman off Luzon, Bogan's TG 38.2, with Third Fleet's two most powerful battleships, would move just east of the San Bernardino Strait approach to the Leyte beachhead. Finally, Halsey said, he would order one of his two other fast carrier task groups to a position off Leyte toward the south in the area of Surigao Strait.

This third force, he said, should be Admiral Davison's TG 38.4—because Davison's group would bring two more battleships into play, including *Washington,* flagship of COMBAT-PAC Adm. Ching Lee. True, TG 38.4 mounted only 207 planes compared to the 326 planes of Admiral McCain's TG 38.1. But TG 38.1 had no battleships, and after *Darter* reported Japanese battleships off Palawan, *Darter's* information was decisive.

Aboard *New Jersey,* Halsey's Third Fleet staff took over the ship's communications setup and installed a teletype machine and pneumatic tube for a fast reliable link between Flag Plot and Radio One, the ship's communication center three decks below. Rollo Wilson had already written out the dispatches implementing Halsey's decisions and now handed them to Communications Liaison Officer Kennie Gifford in Flag Plot. Gifford had already tapped out a teletype to Assistant Communications Officer Charles Fox, in charge of Radio One: "Important messages coming." Now he turned, rolled the papers into a container, and shot them down the pneumatic tube. In Radio One, Fox and his assistant, Lt. Burt Goldstein, stood by with sixteen coding officers and an equal number of radiomen.

Within four minutes the dispatches were encoded. At 0859 the first went out, ordering Davison to turn back from his retirement toward Ulithi. After proceeding west to a point close inshore off Leyte, the message said, Davison's carriers were to launch reinforced searches—teams of bombers and fighters—westward across the southern and central Philippines at dawn on the twenty-fourth. At 0903 Radio One put Wilson's second set of orders on the air. These directed Bogan, as soon as his TG 38.2 completed fueling, to set course for a point just east of San Bernardino Strait and from there launch a reinforced search westward at 0600 on the twenty-fourth across the central Philippines. For Sherman's TG 38.3 no new orders were necessary. By a dispatch earlier that day, at 0252, this task group was positioned east of Luzon and directed to send search planes and a fighter sweep westward over Manila and the northern Philippines at first light on the twenty-fourth. Halsey did not call his fourth carrier group, McCain's TG 38.1, back from its retirement toward Ulithi for one determining reason: he did not expect a major fleet action. This was proved by his act next day, when he saw the Japanese fleet converging from three directions. Then, and only then, he radioed McCain to reverse course and join him at maximum speed.

Thus, as the direct result of *Darter*'s sighting reports, Halsey had set up his Third Fleet forces as follows. By dawn of the twenty-fourth three of his four fast carrier groups would be close inshore along the eastern edge of the Philippines—one just off Luzon, a second close to San Bernardino Strait, and the third close inshore in the vicinity of Surigao Strait. Their dawn searches, fanning out over the entire thousand-mile span of the Philippine archipelago, would lay bare the Japanese naval picture, and spot the targets for Third Fleet's attack. MacArthur and Kinkaid, uneasy about the safety of their men and ships at Leyte, could only have been pleased as they saw how Halsey had disposed his forces.

5

THE SEAFIGHT BEGINS

AND SO IT WAS THAT AS DAWN OF THE TWENTY-THIRD neared, the Battle of Leyte, already set in train by the two submarines' timely sightings south of Palawan, now opened with dawn attacks by *Darter* and *Dace* on the advancing foe. They ran north all night, as that was the direction the Japanese force was taking. They ran at their best surface speed, 19 knots. At first McClintock thought the chase would be as fruitless as his pursuit of other enemy warships the night before. "The tracking party plotted the speed of the force at 22 knots," he noted. But as radar reports began flowing in from *Dace* as well as *Darter*, they soon realized that the Japanese force was not going to outpace them at all. In fact, it seemed to be plodding along at no more than 16 knots and not even zigzagging. On *Dace* Claggett noted, "The targets began to pop up on the screen — we did not have to close their tracks, we just ran with them. For two reasons. First, we had been ordered to get off our contacts before we did anything. You're lucky if you can get them off in an hour. We had to get it on the circuit, and then we had to get someone to receipt for it. That took a little bit of time. So we ran with them while we were getting this off." At 0250 intercept specialists aboard the enemy flagship, we learned long afterward, heard a loud transmission that they were sure came from a submarine nearby. It was McClintock radioing his contact report.

But the big ships made no change in their advance. They

steamed in two columns through the narrow waters of Palawan Passage, the lefthand column slightly in the lead. Destroyers led by light cruisers flanked both columns but no screening ships at all preceded the big ships.

"The second reason we ran with them," said Claggett, "was so that we could be ready to make a periscope attack on them at dawn. We yakked back and forth about this on the voice radio all the time." McClintock, whose submarine had made the first contact, was also the wolfpack leader. His plan, as he wrote it in his patrol report, was: "*Darter* was to attack left flank column first at dawn, with *Dace* about five miles up the track in position to attack the starboard column."

At 0345 McClintock radioed his third contact report. It said, "Both *Darter* and *Dace* may get in. Breaking out oars." By that time the two boats had pulled well in front of their oncoming targets. On both boats everybody was awake and active—the tracking party, the radarmen, the torpedo team. They kept enlarging their estimate of the number of Japanese ships. *Dace's* radar showed first four, then six, then more. "It got up to 20 ships in the middle of the night," said Claggett. In *Darter's* conning tower McClintock "kept looking at that big radar pip just back of the first cruisers"—a battleship, he was sure. He went down to the crew's quarters to tell the coffee drinkers, "We're going to attack the biggest ships of the Japanese fleet in an hour." The biggest ship *Darter* had ever attacked and sunk was a minelayer. Only the night before *Darter* had been left far in the rear by three warships, and the night before that had fired torpedoes at a couple of destroyers without making a hit. "I could see in their eyes that they did not believe me," said McClintock.

Finally Executive Officer Ernie Schwab sounded the buzzer for General Quarters. At that point the target ships were halfway up Palawan Passage, about 90 miles from the northern end. *Darter* and *Dace* had pulled eight miles ahead. *Darter's* patrol report tells what happened next:

With the flagship standing down from Battle Condition to Condition Three, gunners at one of the ten dual five-inch mounts relax while remaining at their station.

0509   Reversed course, headed toward port column and submerged. (*Dace* had just passed us to dive to the northeast.) *Darter* planned to attack from west in half-light of dawn at 0540.

0517   Now light enough to see shapes through scope. We were dead ahead of port flank column of heavy ships. Could not yet identify ships. Visibility was better to west where battleships and cruisers could be seen several thousand yards away. Two destroyers noted to east, both drawing left. There was no echo-ranging.

0517   Swung hard left to open track [for torpedo shots]. It looked as though we might have to fire "down the throat" shots.

0525   Making ready all torpedo tubes, depth ten feet.

0527   Changed course right to parallel column to be able
to fire all ten tubes. Still looked like "down the throat"
shots.

0527   First four ships of column identified as heavy cruisers.
Fifth is probably a battleship.

0528   Range 2880 yards to first cruiser in column. Angle on
the bow is still small.

Then a remarkable thing happened. Until that moment only
the target of the ships' bows advancing straight at him was presented for McClintock's torpedoes. That was what he meant by
"down the throat" shots—short in range perhaps, but head-on
—not much of a target to aim at. But what McClintock could
not know was that at 5:30 A.M. the Japanese formation, speeding up, commenced zigzagging as a dawn precaution. Now,
lucky as *Darter*'s first chance long-range radar contact, came the
submarine's second break—and McClintock ("I got buck
fever") forgot all about his plan to wait to shoot at the battleship at the end of the column.

0532   Target zigged in a 'ships left' to course 350. Got new
setup.

0532   Commenced firing bow tubes at leading cruiser. After
firing two into him and one spread ahead, target was roaring
by so close we couldn't miss, so spread the remainder inside
his length, then swung hard left (to bring stern tubes to bear)
while getting set-up on second cruiser.

0533   Torpedoes started hitting first cruiser. Five hits.
Whipped periscope back to first cruiser to see the sight of a
lifetime. Cruiser was so close that all of her could not be seen
at once with periscope at high power. She was a mass of bil-
lowing black smoke from the number 1 turret to the stern. No
superstructure could be seen. Bright orange flames shot out
from the side along the main deck from the bow to the after
turret. Cruiser was already down by the bow, which was
dipping under. Number 1 turret was at water level. She was

definitely finished. Five hits had her sinking and in flames. It is estimated there were few if any survivors.

By Japanese tradition the force commander sailed in the leading ship, and McClintock, too impatient to wait for the battleship target, had torpedoed the fleet flagship *Atago*. Triple-hulled and supposedly unsinkable, *Atago* plunged beneath the sea at 0653, 18 minutes after five of *Darter's* six torpedoes hit. *Darter's* second spread of torpedoes hit the next cruiser in line. At 0639 the submarine underwent depth charges, but with so many ships swerving in all directions the Japanese counterattack was inaccurate.

Waiting at periscope depth five miles up the track, Commander Claggett saw and heard *Darter's* hits on the second cruiser. As *Dace's* patrol report tells it:

0534 Five more torpedo hits. *Darter* is really having a field day. Can see great pall of smoke completely enveloping spot where ship was at last look. Do not know whether he has sunk but it looks good.

0534 Ship to left is smoking badly. Looks like a great day for the *Darter*. Can see two destroyers making smoke heading for the scene. There is much signaling, shooting of Very stars, etc. It is a great show. The big ships seem to be milling around. I hope they don't scatter too far for me to get in. Light is pretty bad but I have counted eight large ships. . . .

0542 I have now picked a target . . . Range 7000 yards.

0545 Have identified target as heavy cruiser of the *Atagi* or *Nachi* class. There are two of these, but can now see a larger ship astern. Looks like a battleship! Famous statement: "Will let them go by . . . they are only heavy cruisers!" Shifted targets. He is taking evasive action from the *Darter's* position; if he doesn't settle down and present a good set-up, there are two more coming up the line. This is really a submariner's dream . . . sitting right in front of a task force! If I only had some torpedoes aft! After the *Darter's* attack the formation has broken up so that I can't estimate too well how the ships were originally formed, but now with better light conditions I have seen the following: two *Atago* and *Nachi* class cruisers leading battleship or CA (my target); there are two other battleships in column about 1500 yards to eastward and behind my target, presenting a zero angle on bow. There are several destroyers milling around *Darter*'s position about six miles away. There is one large unidentified ship to eastward; this looks like either a carrier or perhaps another battleship; however, I can't make him out very well. Total: eight heavy ships, four destroyers.

0552   The two cruisers passed ahead at about 1500 yards. They were overlapping; appeared to be running screen for my target. Had a beautiful view of them, and identified them positively as *Atago* or *Nachi* class. My target can be seen better now, and appears to be a *Kongo* class battleship. He looks larger than the two cruisers that have just passed ahead. He has two stacks, and superstructure appears much heavier. Sound also reports target screws as heavier and slower than those of cruisers.

0554   Commenced firing a salvo of six bow tubes. Fired One, Two, Three, Four, Five, Six. Took quick look around and saw next battleship still close, so started deep, turning into his wake.

0556   First hit! Second hit! Third hit! Fourth hit!

0601   Heard two tremendous explosions both on sound and through hull. These explosions were apparently magazines as I have never heard anything like it. The sound men said that it sounded as if the bottom of the ocean were blowing up. They were obviously shallow as there was neither any shaking of the boat or water swishing through our superstructure. Nothing could raise this much noise except magazine explosions.

0603   Heard tremendous breaking-up noises—the most gruesome sound I have ever heard. I was at first convinced that it was being furnished by the *Dace* and called for a quick check of all compartments. Noise was coming from the northeast, the direction of the target, and it sounded as if she was coming down on top of us. Comment from the diving officer: "We had better get the hell out of here!"

0605 First depth charge—not close but they got progressively closer, and we received a severe working over the next half hour. Everything not nailed down was knocked loose. But *Dace* was not hurt.

Darter and *Dace* poked up their periscopes for a look around. At 0920 McClintock saw the damaged cruiser dead in the water with three destroyers standing by and three planes circling overhead. For the next four hours he tried to get in range to deliver the finishing blow with his remaining four torpedoes. But every time he got close, the destroyers blocked his way. Unwilling to expend his torpedoes on the destroyers, he decided to trail the cruiser until dark and then team up with *Dace* to finish off the crippled cruiser with a combined attack.

After dark the two submarines surfaced and their skippers talked back and forth by voice radio. They planned a surface attack on the crippled ship but gave this up at 2306 when *Darter*'s radar detector picked up a Japanese radar sweep. Thereupon both *Darter* and *Dace* decided to work around the destroyers and attack from a position ahead of the cruiser, which was now moving slowly back down the channel in the direction it had come from.

Palawan Passage is dangerous water, difficult enough in daytime. The channel between the reefs fringing Palawan Island and the Dangerous Ground to the west is only 25 miles wide and is studded with pinnacles and shoals named for unfortunate sailing ships of the past. *Darter* and *Dace* had been navigating these tricky waters for 24 hours on dead reckoning only. Submerged throughout the day, they could take no sights on the mountains of Palawan. When they surfaced at dusk, clouds prevented taking star sights. To work around the destroyers to an attack position like that from which they had ambushed the fleet in the morning, *Darter* took a circuitous course to the west. At 0105 the boat ran aground on Bombay Shoal with a tremendous crash. The noise evidently registered on the sound gear of one of the Japanese destroyers, which closed to 12,000 yards, only to turn away when presumably it could not figure out what had happened.

Darter was in trouble, bad trouble. McClintock had taken a calculated risk. He knew how hazardous was his end-around maneuver. He knew that clouds and protracted submergence had prevented getting a star sight, and he took a chance going by dead reckoning. The navigational error was narrow, but it was enough. A quarter-knot miscalculation in estimating the current sent *Darter* right across the reef at the hour the tide barely covered it. Flogging on speed at 17 knots, *Darter* piled high on the rock in the dead of night. The reef held it in a relentless clutch. Desperate efforts to get clear were unavailing. Aboard *Darter* confidential papers were burned and secret equipment smashed. The night roared with Japanese aircraft. At any moment a Japanese warship might come lunging from the dark. The submarine was trapped.

In answer to *Darter*'s radio call, *Dace* broke off pursuit of the cruiser. Inching up as close as possible to the stranded *Darter,* *Dace* threw over a line. At high water, 0246, they began trying to pull clear by sallying ship and other devices. None succeeded. At 0345 *Dace,* now no more than 50 yards from *Darter*'s stern, threw over another line. Both submarines broke out their rubber boats and laboriously began transferring the grounded crew. McClintock, sure the enemy would be boarding his boat almost as soon as he left it, cocked an eye at a Japanese ship model kept for recognition-drill purposes on the wardroom sideboard. It was a model of the *Atago.* Grabbing a sheet of paper he scribbled, "Was this the one?" and propped it against the model. Then, last to leave, he climbed into a rubber boat and paddled across to *Dace.*

Before leaving, *Darter's* men rigged demolition charges to go off and explode the torpedo warheads at 0555. At 0550 *Dace's* log noted, "Heard slight explosion but could see no damage." The attempt to blow up *Darter* having failed, Claggett made a try at firing four torpedoes into *Darter's* hull. All struck the reef. *Dace* then pumped thirty four-inch shells into *Darter* along the waterline. By this time it was daylight, and a plane flew over. Dropping their ammunition, *Dace's* gunners scrambled into the conning tower as the hatch slammed and the boat crash-dived. *Dace* escaped because the plane bombed *Darter* instead.

Darter was not easily destroyed. At mid-morning a Japanese destroyer prowled up to the reef and lay to. Planes hovered over the warship, but the precaution was unnecessary because *Dace* was out of torpedoes. Forced to keep *Dace* back at a safe distance, commanders Claggett and McClintock could only watch helplessly while the enemy boarded the stranded sub. Apparently the Japanese took off some communication gear.

That evening Claggett brought *Dace* to the surface and headed his boat toward *Darter,* intending to use his own demolition outfit to put the boat away for keeps. But as *Dace* closed in on *Darter,* enemy "pinging" was heard. It sounded like a Japanese submersible, and the Americans turned to meet this unseen adversary. But nothing more was heard. Late that night, having radioed for help in destroying *Darter, Dace* received permission to leave the area.

Dace went to Australia with *Darter's* crew—eighty-one passengers, including an officer at whose wedding Claggett had stood up as best man and the brother of a *Dace* crewman. That made 165 altogether on board. In such close quarters Claggett could only tell *Darter's* men to pick one place and stay there— except when they had to go to the head.

Meals were brought to them at their places. *Dace* men shared the available bunks with them, and others made do on empty torpedo skids and the like. *Darter's* officers played poker nonstop. Lt. Daniel Wilkinson, the big winner aboard *Darter,* had taken care to fetch along the little book in which he kept score. Resigned, the losers kept losing. Said Ernie Schwab, "The only way I can get a seat in the damned boat is to buy it, and I intend to sit on a cushion from here to Australia no matter how much it hurts my pocketbook." Food ran short, and for the last of the 11-day trip everyone lived on mushroom soup and peanut-butter sandwiches. Claggett said, "I couldn't get Commander McClintock out of my bunk for the rest of the trip except for poker." But as *Dace* exec Mike Benitez said, "We were happy. Few submarines had done what we had done."

While *Dace* continued on to Fremantle, the submarine *Rock* was dispatched to Bombay Shoal to destroy the stranded *Darter*. *Rock* fired ten torpedoes but they only exploded in futile fury against the intervening reef. Finally, on October 31 the Navy's biggest submarine, *Nautilus,* pulled up with orders to destroy *Darter.* Firing point blank, its gunners poured fifty-five six-inch shells into the target. At the end the commander said in his report, "It is doubtful that any equipment in *Darter* would be of value to Japan—except as scrap."

So a valiant submarine came to its end. *Darter* did not lie alone in those dangerous waters off Palawan. Not many miles from *Darter*'s shallow grave lay the deep-buried bones of flagship *Atago,* sent to the bottom by *Darter*'s torpedoes. Nearby lay the remains of yet another Japanese heavy cruiser, torpedoed by *Darter*'s running-mate *Dace.* And the third heavy cruiser, hit by two torpedoes from *Darter,* limped back to Brunei Bay. From there the ship went on to Singapore, where it lay for the rest of the war, paralyzed by a wrecked engine. On the American side, no lives were lost through *Darter*'s grounding. All hands got safely away, jubilant over victory in the opening round of the Battle of Leyte.

6

THE KNOCKOUT THAT WASN'T

ALTHOUGH HE HAD ORDERED DAWN SEARCHES ACROSS THE entire span of the Philippines, at midnight Halsey was already getting ready to hurl his planes at the oncoming heavy Japanese ships. To that end, he was preparing to take tactical command of his fast carrier forces. Not quite satisfied with TG 38.2's search plan for the morrow, he ordered Admiral Bogan to send extra planes along northwest Palawan, along the path taken by the big ships.

He also had thoughts about his force's northern flank. By voice radio our air officer Doug Moulton signaled Bogan: be prepared to have *Independence's* special night-operations air group launch searches to the north at 0000. Midnight passed without the follow-up order. The mission was judged hazardous, and Halsey was pretty sure that if enemy carriers put in an appearance, they would stay beyond the range of our planes and try to take advantage of their Luzon fields by shuttle-bombing: flying on, after striking us, to land and refuel at shore bases, then attempting to bomb us a second time on the way back to their carriers. That was what they had tried to do, using their bases on Saipan and Tinian, in the Battle for the Marianas the previous June, a tactic we were continually on the watch for in Flag Plot.

Also in the night came MacArthur's intelligence warning that the Japanese were staging large numbers of planes into Luzon, and Admiral Kinkaid's resulting dispatch to Seventh Fleet's own carrier force. These were the sixteen jeep carriers operating off Leyte in close support of MacArthur's invasion troops. He ordered them to cancel scheduled troop-support strikes and put the largest CAP over the beachhead to meet the expected bombing attack.

Obviously, to judge from contacts and sightings, still other threatening enemy moves were taking shape north and west of the Philippines. But aboard *New Jersey* we never did figure these out. We didn't know, for instance, that the surface force that had escaped our trap off Formosa had never returned to Japan. This force was ordered to stay poised at the Pescadores west of Formosa, as we learned long afterward, and then — after we landed at Leyte — to head south and join the Japanese fleet's big counterattack.

Confusion was further confounded when *Seadragon* made contact with three ships at night west of Formosa. The submarine mistook the biggest of the warships for an aircraft carrier and claimed a torpedo hit on it. Thereafter commanders from Kinkaid to Mitscher persisted in supposing this the first glimpse of the enemy carriers sure to appear in the developing enemy counterattack. None of us recognized in the scattered contact reports the same, well-identified surface force that had nearly tangled with Third Fleet 2,000 miles to the north a few days before. Even when a long-range patrol plane from Morotai accurately reported three cruisers and five destroyers proceeding southeastward 100 miles west of Manila on the twenty-third, the clue was missed. This force remained unrecognized and unaccounted for from first to last of the Leyte battle. It also escaped with the lightest casualties.

At 0215 we intercepted an important message in Flag Plot: this was *Guitarro's* flash (from the entrance to the Mindoro Strait) of radar contact with a force of fifteen to twenty ships approaching from the west. Thereupon Operations Officer Rollo Wilson woke Admiral Carney. To us this contact could only mean that the big force sighted and attacked by *Darter* and *Dace* was advancing into the central Philippines, without a stop at Manila or Coron Bay. MacArthur's naval chief Kinkaid, holed up inside Leyte Gulf and anxious about getting troops ashore, might still target this big fleet of heavy ships for some sort of "magnified Tokyo Express" rushing in troops, as he continued to do until well into the next day. But to our chief of staff, as we raced to launch searches for these very same ships, what *Guitarro* now reported looked like a formidable Striking Force that had to be smashed before it could get near the Leyte beachhead.

Other night activity was important for the next day's battle. After midnight, long-range radars picked up the distant track of a Japanese reconnaissance plane looking for us. For the first time the night carrier *Independence* went into action. Sending off one of the ship's eighteen radar-equipped Hellcats into the blackness, *Independence*'s fighter director vectored the plane out to intercept the bogey's course. Ens. J. S. Berkheimer lined up the target on his own radar scope and watched the target grow larger as he overtook it. After 25 minutes he looked up from his instruments to see the blue flame of four Mitsubishi engines spitting out of the darkness immediately ahead. Throttling back, he fired a long 50-caliber burst and watched the lumbering plane fall steeply to the left. Without catching fire the big flying boat plunged into the Pacific. At 0229 the whole task group heard Berkheimer's laconic report: "Splash one Emily." An hour later listeners heard him shoot down another four-engine flying boat well to the west of our force.

By contrast, Admiral Sherman's TG 38.3 further north was snooped all night. At 0500, as these carriers closed to 100 miles of Luzon, at least five Japanese planes were on Sherman's radar screen at widely different bearings. At 0530 Admiral Mitscher, aboard his flagship *Lexington* in TG 38.3, warned Sherman on TBS: "Much enemy activity suggests heavy air attack this morning." How right he was.

Our dawn searches on the morning of October 24 went off with a great display of power and prowess. From their positions east of the Philippines the three carrier groups launched a spread of reinforced searches that blanketed the 500 islands and surrounding waters of the Philippine archipelago. In TG 38.2 these scouting teams consisted of a Helldiver and escorting Hellcat in each assigned sector, plus a couple of relay planes sent out to orbit at 100-mile intervals and flash back to us the first contact report as near immediately as possible. TG 38.4's teams were four bombers carrying bombs and four fighters armed with rockets. To the north, TG 38.3 supplemented its sector searches with a fifty-fighter sweep launched at enemy airfields in the Manila area, where heavy reinforcements had been flown in from the north and from where Mitscher rightly expected an attack might come. Dawn fighter sweeps were a Mitscher specialty and worked especially well on Formosa, stifling enemy interception and helping to establish control of the air for the rest of the day.

On board *New Jersey* that morning excitement mounted. All our antennae pointed west. Listeners guarded every air communication frequency. Flag Plot's ears were glued to the wavelengths that linked the fleet's ships with the pilots now boring west through morning mists over the Sibuyan Sea. What would they find? Transports? Flattops? The superbattleships our Navy had heard about all through the war but never laid eyes on? Was the Japanese fleet at last coming out to fight? It was essential to find out, to find the targets and attack them at the earliest possible moment.

At 0730 no word had yet reached us. In Flag Plot tension grew. The place was noisy, crowded. Bill Kitchell, Halsey's flag lieutenant, borrowed headphones to try intercepting the searchers' report direct. Halsey, Carney, and a dozen others listened to the pilots' voices piped into the room on loudspeakers. Men kept looking at their watches and saying, "It's about time." They laughed and groaned at the pilots' chatter: "Solid overcast

at Cebu—I can't see a thing." "My radio is out—can you hear
me?"

At 0820 Lt. Bill Verity of *Cabot* raised a shout that everybody heard: "I see 'em." He reported the Japanese formation on
an easterly course off Mindoro Island. "Big ships," he yelled.
Two minutes later the voice of Cdr. Mort Eslick of *Intrepid's*
Bombing 18 came on—relayed loud, clear, and very cool: "Four
battleships, eight heavy cruisers and 13 destroyers, course east,
off the southern tip of Mindoro."

It was the sighting of the day. Others would be more start-
ling, but none so timely and accurate. No transports among the
big ships—that was important. And no carrier—that settled a
question, too. Eslick was off on the number of battleships—
there were five; and on the total number of ships—there were
then 28. But he had told Halsey just what Halsey needed to
know, namely, that the major surface strength of the Japanese
fleet, assembled in the largest armada seen massed together in
the entire war, was advancing in broad daylight into striking
range of Third Fleet's carrier-plane attack. Said Mick Carney,
"Never in any main action at sea has the intelligence information from searching been so good, so thorough, so quickly put
through, and so complete." Would that we could have said the
same later in the engagement.

Attack was Halsey's style. Left to himself he would probably
not have waited for the enemy force to come to him but ordered our battleships forward to meet them. He had been told
not to send any ships through the San Bernardino Strait without Nimitz's say-so and he knew Nimitz would never agree because the channel might be mined. Even so, the Japanese were
advancing toward him as they had not advanced since the Battle of Midway in 1942, and within minutes Halsey ordered all
three carrier groups to concentrate on our TG 38.2 off the strait
and launch attacks.

This was not to be. Our dawn searches actually found *two*
enemy surface forces. TG 38.4's armed searches were virtu-

ally armed strikes, and at 0905 the planes from *Enterprise* and *Franklin* flying over the southern sector found and attacked a force of seven warships including two battleships headed across the Sulu Sea in the direction of Surigao Strait. They reported bomb and rocket hits, including a bomb burst on the stern of a battleship. It took a little time to unscramble this report. But then in Flag Plot the thought came to us at once: a coordinated attack organized to hit our landing force from south and north!

Admiral Halsey's reaction was to dismiss this southern formation as the lesser force, to be handled by the old battle-wagons and cruisers lent Kinkaid's Seventh Fleet for the Philippines operation.

From Hawaii this same morning Admiral Nimitz sent us an ULTRA tip from radio intercepts: "Commander First Mobile Fleet unlocated but estimated in the Formosa–Philippine Sea area." This was the chief of the Japanese carrier force, and the telltale sign for the Pearl Harbor decoders was the including of this command as addressee on messages concerning southward moves of its replenishment tankers. That, said Nimitz, strongly supported the judgment that the carriers had departed Japan for the south. Our intelligence chief, Mike Cheek, at once wrote Carney a little note: Nimitz's estimate could only indicate that this high Japanese commander with an unknown number of carriers and attending vessels had put to sea in the direction of Third Fleet. Moulton, more vehement, said the enemy carriers must be found, and Halsey agreed. At 0846 the admiral sent the following orders to TG 38.1: Break off retirement to Ulithi, rendezvous in mid-ocean to the northwest at dawn October 25. Moulton, still insistent, then wrote Halsey's second message, radioed at 0855 to Mitscher in TG 38.3 off Luzon: "Carriers not located. Keep area to north under observation."

No way. Our ships were too far apart for voice radio communication and Third Fleet's message reached Mitscher's flagship only at 1130. Even had Mitscher received the word earlier, there was no way he could respond. He could not even respond to Halsey's directive to concentrate off San Bernardino Strait. Their night snoopers having found TG 38.3 but not 38.2, the Japanese had identified TG 38.3 as the entire American carrier fleet—and TG 38.3 ships were subjected to such heavy assaults by attackers flying from nearby Luzon that the force could not even respond to Halsey's order to join the attack on the big ships advancing into the Sibuyan Sea. Mitscher had time only to respond: "Many planes around."

Just as TG 38.3 carriers poised to launch their eighty-plane strike, alarms sounded. Air raid! Radars in *Essex*'s CIC showed not one but two waves of attackers closing from Luzon—first a forty-plane bogey and right behind it another of equal size. From his flagship *Lexington* Mitscher shot off his "Hey Rube" signal, the old circus call for help, peremptorily recalling the sixty fighters from their sweep over Manila. They broke off just as they sighted in on a lot of twin-engine bombers streaming in to land, apparently from Formosa. They raced back to base, but too late to join the fight.

Having already sent off so many fighters, TG 38.3 had to scramble for interceptors. *Langley*'s twelve CAP planes over the force had already shot down four intruders and the fight had not even started.

At 0800 TG 38.3 commander Frederick Sherman ordered his four carriers to launch every fighter aboard, including those to accompany the deckload strike. Aboard *Princeton* Capt. W. H. Buracker ordered all torpedo bombers struck below to make way for the fighters. Standing on the catapult on *Essex*'s flight deck was Air Group Commander David McCampbell's Hellcat. McCampbell was to have flown as flight coordinator of TG 38.3's opening strike on the big ships. Now he took off as the first of eight *Essex* fighter pilots scrambled to head off the incoming wave of attackers. All told, some forty-two Hellcats rose from the four flight decks in the emergency. A dozen *Princeton* fighters had a head start but somehow they missed contact. It was McCampbell and his handful of *Essex* Hellcats, vectored out on a 250 bearing, who tallyhoed.

Pouring on the power at 18,000 feet, they ran into a formation of at least sixty Japanese fighters, bombers, and torpedo planes. Sizing up the situation fast, the Hellcats began to work over the enemy from the top down. The Japanese bombers dove through the overcast and escaped. Pulled away from the planes they were supposed to protect, the Japanese fighters went into a tight circle that left no opening for attack. McCampbell, veteran of South Pacific and Marianas air battles, knew all about this maneuver. It was a Lufbery weave, invented by a First World War pilot to keep the enemy off your tail. McCampbell and his wingman, Ken Rushing, calmly maintained their altitude advantage and waited for the circle to break up. When it did, they pounced. Said McCampbell:

> In the next hour or so we followed the formation of the weaving fighters, taking advantage of every opportunity to knock off those who attempted to climb to our altitude, scissored outside, straggled or became too eager and came to us singly. In all we made 18 or 20 passes, being very careful not to expose ourselves and to conserve ammunition by withholding our fire until within very close range. After following the decimated formation nearly all the way to Manila — there were 18 enemy planes left in the formation when we broke off—we returned, nearly exhausted of ammunition and so near fuel exhaustion we had barely enough gas to taxi out of the arresting gear.

McCampbell shot down nine planes, his wingman six, and the other *Essex* pilots got nine between them, a total of twenty-four. For this decisive interception, McCampbell won one of the two Medals of Honor awarded to Navy men in the Battle of Leyte.

As early as 0805 a third large raid appeared on the screen from 60 miles to the west. At 0831 Sherman ordered *Lexington* to scramble the task group's twelve remaining fighters. In *Essex's*

CIC, reports of enemy planes kept coming in. Once the interceptors shouted tallyho, it was impossible to give them further direction, and the bogeys were so big that the fighter directors sent every plane aloft into action. Everything happened so fast that by the time the fighters that were "Hey Rubed" over Manila whizzed back over the force the bogeys had already disappeared.

Many of the bombers that ducked into the clouds when our interceptors dived at them never succeeded in locating Sherman's flattops and ended up straggling back to Luzon. At least three times during the morning Sherman, veteran of the Coral Sea battle, maneuvered his ships under timely rain squalls. At 0939 TG 38.3 pulled out to the edge of a squall to land fighters that needed reservicing. At that moment there was no bogey on the screen nearer than 50 miles away. Suddenly a lone Japanese bomber glided down out of the clouds over the light carrier *Princeton* and dropped a 250-kilogram bomb that penetrated the ship's flight deck amidships, exploded in the bakeshop and singed the hangar deck, which set gasoline afire. The flames licked through the open bomb-bay doors on six Avengers, enveloping their torpedoes, which exploded one by one, sending the forward elevator mast-high and blowing the other elevator onto the flight deck. Great efforts were made but *Princeton* could not be saved. When later in the day the cruiser *Birmingham* pulled alongside to help fight the fires, a tremendous explosion on the carrier sent fragments flying that killed 229 and wounded 420, almost everybody topside on the cruiser. "A spectacle terrible to behold," said an officer. "Blood ran freely down our waterways."

TG 38.4 to the south also ran into delays responding to Halsey's directive to concentrate on our TG 38.2 and add its strength to the attack on the advancing big ships. Admiral Davison's search-strikes had found and attacked the southern force. Still another of his armed searches found and attacked two destroyers near Negros in the central Philippines. Not until these planes were recovered could Davison's carriers move northward.

All this left it up to Admiral Bogan's TG 38.2 to carry the attack to the advancing Japanese surface force. Because *Bunker Hill* had been sent back to Manus and *Independence* was reserved for night action, TG 38.2 fielded only two carriers and packed much less hitting power than any other of Task Force 38's four groups. That scarcely entered our minds in Flag Plot as Admiral Bogan at 0837 went on TBS to tell Halsey that he had forty-five planes all set on *Intrepid* and *Cabot* to launch against the ships his searchers had just located. Halsey's reply: "Strike rpt strike!" This was greeted with cheers on all the ships of the force. Everybody caught the resounding echo of his famous radio to his beleaguered carriers as he took command at Noumea in the South Pacific's darkest hours: "Attack repeat attack."

In Flag Plot excitement only intensified. We guarded all the air frequencies. Stan Massie on channel C heard Bill Ellis, the strike coordinator from *Intrepid,* collect his birds — twenty-one Hellcats, twelve Helldivers, nine torpedo-carrying Avengers — above our ships and wing west. Dick Taylor on channel A tuned in on the relay planes taking their station at 20,000 feet along the way.

We had a devil of a time that morning untangling garbled reports of TG 38.4's doings to the south. And TG 38.3 was too far north for us to get any sense of their running fight at that early hour. But we had no trouble hearing from our own attackers. In Flag Plot we heard Ellis leading his planes somewhat north of west, bypassing the nest of Japanese airfields at Cebu. And then we heard Ellis reporting over the target.

At 1026 he saw the enemy force, by now well out into the Sibuyan Sea. He could see the formation clearly, though clouds formed a broken layer at 5,000 feet. And what a sight! Never before had Americans laid eyes on the superbattlewagons *Yamato* and *Musashi,* bigger than our supers *Iowa* and *New Jersey* and fitted, we had heard, with 18.1-inch guns that could shoot further than our 16-inchers. Huge pagoda-like masts towered above the armored decks of these behemoths. Abristle with 110 guns, five-inchers in their secondary batteries and machine guns sticking out from almost every corner of their superstructure, these battleships could throw up a wall of antiaircraft fire. Ellis reported them advancing in company with three other battleships, eight heavy cruisers, and many screening destroyers. They were moving in two formations about seven miles apart.

As our planes drew near, the warships below went into two circular formations—the standard Japanese disposition for AA defense—and let fly. Black patches, white phosphorus-chains, red tracers filled the sky. Antiaircraft fire, all our pilots reported, was intense. But wonder of wonders, no fighters appeared to contest the attack. So out of the sun our dive bombers hurtled down through the flak. As they released their thousand-pounders and pulled out, huge geysers erupted around the big ships. The Japanese at this point were in the open waters of the Sibuyan Sea and had room to twist and turn, to evade the bombers. At the same time, though, the torpedo planes, gliding in from the east, skimmed low over the water to press home their lethal attack. Their leader, Bill Van Antwerp, said afterward, "I saw that damned pagoda. But it was the size of the ship that got me. It was so long you couldn't miss." And he didn't. Van Antwerp dropped his deadly fish only 900 yards from a superbattleship as it started its ponderous turn. His torpedo exploded on the ship's forward bow. Three minutes later, under cover of strafing runs by Hellcat fighters, eight Avengers from the light carrier *Cabot* followed their leader Randy McPherson through a wall of AA fire. The plane just behind McPherson wobbled, tilted sharply to the right, and, smoke pouring from its engine, slammed into the water. The others pressed on toward a cruiser three ships back from the superbattleship. McPherson's torpedo caught the 20,000-ton warship amidships and blew a hole at the waterline. The cruiser lost speed and Ellis, watching and taking pictures high overhead, saw it drop out of the formation. One other torpedo plane fell to the ships' guns; all the rest of the strike force returned safely, as shipboard ACIs exultantly reported to us that same morning.

A good start, and Commander Ellis was still over the target as TG 38.2's second strike arrived — twelve fighters, twelve dive bombers, and nine torpedo planes. Ellis had flashed word that no enemy planes were around to interfere. And the weather was even better. The clouds had parted. Once again Ellis sent the Helldivers plunging down in near-vertical dives at the two superbattleships in the lead formation as the ships turned to evade. The bombers saw two hits on one of the big ships. The Avengers, flashing out of the east, bored through the flak, flew right over the masts of a big cruiser, and put three torpedoes into the side of what appeared to be the same superbattleship. One tore a hole in the big ship's bow. The ship kept station, but the whole formation was seen to slow its advance.

At about 1100 Admiral Sherman's TG 38.3, still fighting a bad fire on *Princeton* as we now heard, shook off enough attackers and recovered enough fighters to join the onslaught. Arriving over the big ships in the Sibuyan Sea at 1330, they found the target vessels milling around, and a battleship of the *Yamato* class, with another warship in company, lagging behind the rest. In the eighty-three-plane attack, the biggest of the day, even the fighters unloaded 500-pound bombs. Results were mixed. Returning pilots claimed hits on two heavy cruisers and one battleship. Somehow the seventeen "torpeckers" of Air Group 11 had been sent off armed not with torpedoes but with lighter bombs. Strike Coordinator Hugh Winters of *Lexington,* who had protested this decision, had to signal that he had seen no "lucky hit on a heavy ship's magazine," and his estimate of damage from high overhead was "poor" due to the obscuring clouds.

Even before these planes left the target, another big attack group arrived—from TG 38.4—to deliver that group's first strike at the big ships. Launched at 1313 off Samar, sixty-five planes from Admiral Davison's four flattops executed a well-coordinated attack at 1415. Once again no enemy planes opposed them, and this time some of the target ships fired their main batteries trying to fend off low-flying torpedo planes. Cdr. Joe Kibbe, *Franklin's* air group commander, shouted that his outfit had hit one of the superbattleships with "at least four bombs" and from one to three torpedoes. Another bomb was seen to make a hit on the forward deck of the other super-battleship. He also said that Lt. (jg) Bob Ransom of *Franklin's* Torpedo Squadron 13 had sunk a light cruiser. This was the cruiser hit in the bow just as it turned the other way, causing the ship to roll so crazily that pilots saw it roll over and disappear beneath the waves. *Enterprise's* strike leader Dan Smith reported bomb and torpedo hits on one of the two Japanese superbattleships, and damage to a cruiser and two destroyers. Two of the bombs were seen to hit a heavy cruiser that seemed to be screening the more heavily damaged superbattleship.

Our TG 38.2's third strike, fifteen fighters, twelve dive bombers, and three torpedo planes, launched at 1350, was the last of the day. Pilots saw what they took to be two battleships lagging behind the main force, one listing and afire. Driving in relentlessly, the torpedo planes sent yet another fish into the side of the crippled ship, which they described as a *Yamato*-class superbattleship. Pilots and gunners from three different returning bombers told of seeing an explosion on a heavy cruiser and said that after smoke cleared away the cruiser had vanished from sight.

At 1518 Admiral Bogan told Halsey on TBS that while the enemy ships circled when under attack, they still seemed to keep their easterly course. I had been on duty at our standup desk as the last of these attackers reached the target. I heard the flash report relayed from the strike coordinator. His final report: the ships were reversing course. At this a shout went up in Flag Plot: "We've stopped 'em." The Japanese were turning back under our day-long onslaught!

After the planes returned to their carriers. Bogan's ACI officers sent us a flash report. After describing the condition of the stricken superbattleship during the sixth and last attack, they added, "The enemy's course to the west may be retiring or may be protection of the cripples." Shortly afterward we received Admiral Davison's report on TG 38.4's afternoon strike: "Enemy force on easterly course at first strike. When last seen, on westerly course."

By that time John Marshall was at our Flag Plot post. A blizzard of reports of enemy damage had reached our stand. The enemy had taken a beating all day—not to mention two cruisers sunk and a third forced to drop back the day before. A quick count established that at midday yet another cruiser was no longer present—possibly the cruiser that Ellis had seen drop out of the formation after the morning strike. Our first reckoning showed that a total of 261 Third Fleet planes had hammered the big ships in six successive strikes. That was nothing like the 1,000-plane attacks Halsey threw in the opening days of his western Pacific campaign. But this time our attackers met with no interference from interceptors aloft.

At our Flag Plot post we knew personally the ACIs who had received and evaluated the innumerable hits reported by our returning airmen. We believed that the enemy warships had taken a whale of a beating. We were inclined to believe the damage reports. Had the Japanese force indeed been stopped and forced to retire?

At day's end we sent off to Nimitz and MacArthur, information copy to King in Washington, this report of action against the big Japanese surface ships:

Main Body reversed course to 270 about 1400 when 30 miles east of Tablas Island and while again being attacked. Score from incomplete reports: one *Yamato* class bombed torpedoed left afire and down at bow. *Kongo* class two bomb hits left smoking and apparently badly damaged. Bomb hits on one or both remaining battleships. Two torpedo hits on one of these bombed battleships. One light cruiser torpedoed and capsized. Torpedo hits on two heavy cruisers and bomb hits on another heavy cruiser. Night air attack probable.

7

THE JAPANESE CARRIERS ARRIVE

LUCK HELPED US SPOT THE ENEMY SURFACE FLEET ADvancing to destroy our invasion to retake the Philippines. Luck deserted us when we tried to find the enemy carriers sent forth for the same purpose.

A submarine wolfpack led by *Besugo* was set to watch the Bungo channel from Japan's Inland Sea. But after lurking for days where Japanese warships might be expected to sortie, *Besugo* was given permission to stalk a convoy. So the enemy carriers sailed for the south unseen. Next our long-legged reconnaissance planes from Saipan missed their southward passage along the extreme limit of their coverage. Our radio intelligence was able, deducing from messages ordering their tankers to southern rendezvous, to send estimates that the enemy carriers were probably at sea. But where? About this time the submarine *Hammerhead* made contact by night with a formation of enemy warships northwest of Manila. The skipper not only identified an aircraft carrier among them but attacked it and (erroneously) claimed a torpedo hit. This led commanders from MacArthur to Mitscher to look for the enemy carrier force west rather than east of the Philippines.

Halsey, east of the Philippines, had to be watchful of his flank, so when Nimitz's intercept intelligence estimated that the enemy carriers had departed Japan October 20, he paused momentarily amid the opening hours of Third Fleet's big air attacks on the surface force to send this message at 0855 to Mitscher in the northernmost of his three carrier groups: "Enemy carrier strength not located. Keep area to north under observation."

Mitscher received this message at 1125. By this time TG 38.3 had fought off three waves of shore-based air attacks from Luzon, had suffered a disabling hit on the light carrier *Princeton,* and had already sent aloft most of its intercepting fighters. It wasn't until 1100 that TG 38.3 had a chance to launch its first deck-load strike against the big ships in the Sibuyan Sea, and it wasn't until 1155 that its commander, Admiral Sherman, had enough fighters to provide escort for the searchers to be sent north as Halsey had directed.

This search was to launch right along with a second deck-load strike against the big surface ships at 1245. But after air attackers coming from the west all morning, a new threat appeared from the opposite direction. Another large group of enemy planes appeared on the radar screen 105 miles out and closing from the northeast. Thereupon Admiral Sherman canceled the search, sent off the strike in a rush, and scrambled twenty-three fighters from *Lexington* and *Langley,* including those assigned to the search.

These Hellcats met the enemy planes about 45 miles from the force and broke up the attack. In all they claimed eleven planes shot down, and the rest ducked away. While the dogfight was still going on, *Lexington*'s radar detected another large group of enemy planes 90 miles away and closing—once again from the northeast. More fighters were scrambled and intercepted the raid about 25 miles from the force. These Japanese fliers gave a better account of themselves, and some broke through. Lt. Dan Morris of *Essex*'s Fighting 15, said, "The enemy pilots were the most aggressive encountered since the fleet action of 19 June. They flew excellent formation, kept good sections and traded head-on shots. They evidently were part of the No. 1 team."

Some attackers filtered through. At 1458 lookouts on Sherman's flagship sighted a flaming plane through clouds some 10 miles away. Moments later five carrier-type planes—identified as Judys—broke out of the clouds and dived on *Essex*. All five dropped bombs that landed from 100 to 300 yards from the big flattop. One, hit by the ship's AA fire, veered sharply and plunged into the sea just beyond the destroyer screen. At 1544 another Judy swooped on *Lexington*, dropped a bomb that missed astern, and made off through the clouds toward Luzon.

The attack, ineffectual though it was, left Sherman, as he said later, "strongly suspicious of the presence of Japanese carriers to the northeast." He asked and received Mitscher's permission to launch the delayed search without waiting to give them fighter escort. At 1305 *Lexington* sent off five Helldivers to search sectors to the north and east to a distance of 350 miles.

At the time Mitscher and TG 38.3 were too far to the north for us to intercept their TBS and air frequency communications. All through this day of incessant attacks on our northern group, we knew only what came to us by wireless. Thus at 1207 Mitscher radioed a flash report to Halsey recounting morning searches, the shooting down of 100 attacking planes, the heavy damage to *Princeton*. This message, received on our flagship at 1331, also added this cryptic item: "Large bogey from northeast approaching to attack. Searchers to north launched at 1305."

That was Halsey's first inkling that enemy carriers might have arrived in the area. But that was all. Many exchanges passed among Mitscher, Sherman, and their force in the next hours, but we were in the dark. At 1540 two of their searchers reported their first sighting—a force of surface ships at 18 10N 125 30E. An hour later, another pilot "got a good look" at the carrier force somewhat to the north of the first sighting: "four carriers, two light cruisers, five destroyers." It was this evaluated report relayed by Mitscher, sent at 1717, that reached Halsey at 1730, and finally gave him something firm on which to make the judgments that confronted him. The one thing clear at that late hour, as Mitscher and Sherman had already agreed, was that it was too late in the day to launch an attack and action would have to await the morning. The actual dispatch from Mitscher read as follows: "New contact: Afternoon search reports 3 CV 4 to 6 CA and 6 DD at 18 10N 125 30E which is 180 miles east of Aparri [at north tip of Luzon]. One of CVs is of ISE class. On course 110 speed 15 knots."

With that, Halsey's information was at last complete. He would now have to decide where next to hurl the power of Third Fleet's attack—and he would have to decide fast.

8

DECISION

At midday on the twenty-fourth Admiral Carney made this estimate of the situation:

Major forces of the Japanese fleet were moving toward a predetermined geographical and time focus, and the earliest concentration would be on October 25, although the exact physical objective was not yet clear.

It seemed clear enough to us at the intelligence desk that the two enemy surface forces were advancing via the two straits to strike the Leyte beachhead in a combined assault. Later Admiral Carney said he couldn't be sure that the heavy ships advancing toward San Bernardino Strait might not suddenly shorten their charge toward Leyte Gulf by bypassing the strait and ducking instead through the narrow passage west of Samar leading to Leyte.

At that moment the big surface force was continuing its advance in the teeth of our almost unremitting carrier-plane attacks. At the same time Admiral Halsey knew from orders radioed by Admiral Kinkaid that MacArthur's Navy was getting set to deal with the lesser surface force headed toward Leyte via the Surigao Strait.

As to the suspected missing enemy carrier force, there was some confusion. On Admiral Mitscher's flagship, fighting off heavy air attacks to the north, the staff began to think, especially after a carrier-type plane bombed *Princeton,* that the carriers coming down from Japan might be poised west of Luzon and shuttle-bombing us, using Luzon bases to attack our carriers while operating from flight decks safely outside our range. For his part Admiral Halsey, as he said later, "could see that a major coordinated enemy movement was under way." But as the afternoon of October 24 began, "the expected enemy carrier force was missing from the picture." It might have been lurking west of the Philippines, as Mitscher and others seemed to think. Or it might have been closing from the north, where Halsey had asked Mitscher to search early that morning.

But the big surface ships at that point kept coming onward, closer and closer, on a path leading to the Leyte beachhead, and Halsey had to be ready to meet them if necessary. So at 1512 his operations officer Rollo Wilson sent out an alerting message to all ships concerned: Task Force 34 would be formed under Commander Battle Line, Admiral Lee. The dispatch, headed "Battle Plan," said, "Task Force 34 engages decisively at long ranges." And it said Admiral Davison commanding TG 38.4 would "conduct carriers of his group and TG 38.2" off San Bernardino Strait "clear of surface fighting." And Halsey himself would be OTC—officer in tactical command—in *New Jersey*. This order was only provisional, but as late as 1710, when Davison brought his carriers within voice-radio range, Halsey sent him this message: "Operate in this vicinity until further orders. Keep [carrier] groups concentrated. If enemy sorties, Task Force 34 will be formed when directed by me."

And that was the projected fleet disposition when finally at 1730 a dispatch from Mitscher brought decisive word to Flag Plot that the missing Japanese carriers had at last been found and conclusively identified. That, as Halsey said, "completed the picture."

It certainly did.

So fierce was the shore-based air onslaught on TG 38.3 that morning that its carriers had no chance until after noon to launch the early strike on the heavy ships that Halsey asked for.

And then it had been delayed again when Admiral Sherman's planes had to beat back two more waves of attacking planes—this time by carrier-type planes closing from the northeast. So the expected enemy carriers had put in their appearance where Halsey expected them—and got in the first licks.

It took time for Mitscher to get all this straight. Sherman had sent Helldivers without fighter escort to look northward for the enemy carriers. But there was confusion. At 1510 one sighted a surface force but no carriers. Only at 1610 did a TG 38.3 searcher find carriers maneuvering some 60 to 100 miles further north. And it wasn't until, back at their ships, the "pilots who got good looks" reported the enemy ships sailing in two formations that Mitscher was able to give us the picture: in the second group were "two *Zuikaku*-class carriers and one light carrier" (actually there were four in all) along with attending warships. And by this time information filtering through told us the enemy had indeed arrived undetected, had struck twice —and were still unscathed. Yet John Lawrence, drawing up Third Fleet's action report of the day's fighting, reflected some uncertainty on this point.

The dispatch, initialed by Admiral Carney and addressed to Nimitz and MacArthur, summed up the day's action that led to the decision Halsey now made—the dawn search-strikes that found two powerful surface forces in pincer movement toward Leyte, the Luzon-based enemy air raids on TG 38.3, our day-long onslaught and seeming repulse of the enemy's Main Body ("Main Body score from incomplete reports: 1 *Yamato* bombed torpedoed afire down by bow, one battleship left smoking apparently badly damaged, one light cruiser torpedoed capsized"). At the end Lawrence inserted Mitscher's report of the late carrier-force sighting and added, still tentatively, "Planes from this force may have been attacking TG 38.3 prior to contact."

Late or not, Halsey's "missing piece of the picture" had been found. And here at last was the target Halsey had sought ever since he went to sea again. Our reach for the Philippines had brought the enemy carriers out, and brought them within our range.

In every battle of the Pacific war, carriers had been decisive. In every engagement it was vital to hit first. The enemy had struck first. Still intact, they must be attacked. They must be annihilated. For Halsey there could be no alternative. We had the force to overwhelm them. Closing on them in the night, we might even surprise them. At dawn our carriers could crush them. And what's more, for the first time none of them would get away. Task Force 34's battlewagons, already alerted, would rush forward to finish them off. Knock off the carriers and we can operate freely off Tokyo. Destroy them and Japan's fate is sealed.

A swift consultation followed in Flag Plot. Moulton, who had called for the morning search, now argued that the day's delay played into our hands: with TG 38.1 already rushing back to a hurry-up mid-ocean fueling rendezvous at dawn, a combined attack by all of Third Fleet's twelve fast carriers would slaughter them. Stassen said knock off the carriers now and MacArthur won't have to worry about them anymore when he makes his next scheduled moves in retaking the Philippines in December and January.

Attack was Halsey's way. All day his airmen attacked, attacked, and attacked the big Japanese surface ships. His message to Nimitz and MacArthur repeated the first flash reports of heavy damage. Halsey was inclined to accept them. He had heard the pilots' final report that as they left the target the enemy ships had turned back. Assistant Air Officer Jack Hoerner said that in six strikes our planes had exploded so many bombs topside on the warships that their guns could no longer shoot with any precision. Operations Officer Rollo Wilson said Third Fleet could not stand passively waiting around to see whether the battered enemy would venture through the strait. That, he said, would be like watching a rathole. There were ships to hit that had not been hit. The carriers!

Halsey knew what he wanted. Get the carriers! No one in this swift consultation seems to have posed options. Carney, who was to say years later, "I might have had other ideas," did not. Chief of Third Fleet's vaunted "dirty tricks department," Carney was brilliantly successful with many of his ideas. He was quick, and this time he saw quickly what should be done. The carriers, the deciding force in every engagement of the war so far, were out there, still unscathed, with this capacity to shuttle-bomb us, as Carney had seen them try to do at Saipan, Tinian, and Guam. Gen. Bill Riley, the level-headed plans officer and just the man to bring up alternatives, missed the meeting. Intelligence Officer Mike Cheek was not consulted. Neither was Radio Intelligence Officer Gil Slonim, who had been listening for radio intercepts all day and heard about the meeting only afterward.

Could not Halsey have left Task Force 34 to guard San Bernardino Strait with one of his groups providing air cover? Several of Halsey's commanders on their flagships, including Ching Lee himself, expected him to do so. Carney always held it a cardinal rule never to divide the fleet in battle—although nobody countered that the force Halsey disposed of was so huge it amounted to several fleets. For Halsey the prospect that beckoned was the chance he had planned for ever since he left Manus, and now that it loomed before him he was not going to miss it: the chance to throw both the fast carriers and the fast battleships at the enemy and wipe out their carrier force once and for all.

Probably no argument could have held Halsey back. "Here's where we're going, Mick," he told Carney, sweeping his arm across the big Flag Plot chart toward the north. Carriers, battleships, and all.

And then the orders went out: at 2006 to TG 38.1, "Proceed at best speed toward Point Mick (rendezvous)"—and see Mitscher's dispatch reporting enemy carriers position to the north. At 2009 to TGs 38.2 and 38.4: "Head north." And at

2022 to Mitscher, information all group commanders: "At 2300 Groups 38.2 and 38.4 pass through 14 28N 125 50E course 000 speed 25 knots. Upon joining Commander TF 38 take charge all three groups attack enemy carrier force. Keep CTG 38.1 advised your movements. He is herewith directed join you earliest."

These orders sent, Commander Third Fleet next addressed an urgent dispatch at 2024 to Kinkaid, Commander Seventh Fleet, to the south. The message contained no suggestion that the warships his forces had attacked all day were turning back: "Enemy force Sibuyan sea 1925 position 12 45N 122 40E course 120 speed 12 knots. Strike reports indicate enemy heavily damaged. Am proceeding north with three groups to attack enemy carrier force at dawn."

Decision made, Halsey had already turned in.

9

DISSENT

MY ROOMMATE, LT. HARRIS COX, JUST LEAVING OUR STAND-up desk in Flag Plot, witnessed this decision. He was appalled. Back in our room he exclaimed, Halsey has just done what the Japanese hoped he would.

For days, seated in our quarters, Harris had been studying a rare captured document that came aboard when we stopped at Ulithi October 6. Time and again I watched and heard him puzzling over this twenty-eight-page translation. It was no routine bit of captured intelligence. It was nothing less than the Japanese Navy's Z-Plan for throwing back expected American invasions.

Never before had we laid eyes on anything like this. And only the most improbable series of events delivered it into our hands at this hour.

In Admiral Yamamoto's heyday, the conquering Japanese had felt no need to draw up large-scale defensive plans. But after an ULTRA radio-intercept tipoff in 1943 knocked Yamamoto out of the war, the scene changed. The "Arsenal of Democracy" back home was turning out a big new Navy that soon bypassed Japanese strongholds like Rabaul and Truk, and staged successive leapfrogging invasions that brought us ever nearer the Japanese homeland. The initiative having clearly passed to the Americans, it became the lot of Yamamoto's successor, Admiral

Koga, at Imperial Navy headquarters in Tokyo, to develop the first comprehensive, detailed Japanese defensive plan.

It was this vital document that came into our possession just before the big seafight for Leyte, and once again the death of the supreme Japanese naval chief in an air crash played its fateful part. Admiral Koga, Yamamoto's successor, also met death when his flight miscarried. This occurred on March 31, 1944, when he and his staff set out to establish a shore command at Davao in the southern Philippines. Two big flying boats took off from Palau (a third was delayed) but ran into heavy weather. Admiral Koga's plane disappeared into the sea, never to be found. The second was wrecked trying to make a midnight landing in shallow water off the central Philippine island of Cebu. All of the eleven who reached shore, including Admiral Fukudome, Admiral Koga's badly injured chief of staff, were taken prisoner by Filipino guerrillas. And in the wreckage of the plane the Filipinos found important papers, including a document bound in red. These papers were soon in the hands of Col. James Cushing, chief of guerrilla forces in Cebu. He recognized their importance and arranged for a submarine, *Crevalle,* to carry them back to MacArthur's headquarters in Australia. Allied Intelligence in Brisbane quickly translated the twenty-eight-page document, which bore the legend, "Z Operation Orders: Secret Fleet Orders Operation No. 73, dated 8 March 1944, aboard flagship *Musashi* at Palau, by Koga Mineichi, commander-in-chief of the Combined Fleet."

One copy of this document went to Admiral Nimitz's headquarters in Pearl Harbor, where it caught the attention of intelligence officers Eddie Layton and Jasper Holmes. They immediately sought and won MacArthur's permission to make further copies. One of these copies fell into our hands when Third Fleet put in at Ulithi for replenishment and mail.

The Z-Plan, drawn up before our invasion of the Marianas in June 1944, was the master matrix for subsequent Japanese defense plans, including the A-Plan and the SHO-Plan, used, as we learned much later, for defense of the Philippines. This first master defense plan set forth how the Navy would meet invasions wherever our side might attack—in the north Pacific, in the Marianas, and even in the Indian Ocean. The plan went into greatest detail to stress the important role of land-based air as the Japanese fell back from the central Pacific with its tiny islets to the larger islands nearer Japan and the Asian mainland. For the Combined Fleet four broad options were set forth —first, when the whole fleet went into action; second, when the carrier force would operate ahead of a separately attacking Main Body of surface ships; third, when the carriers' planes would strike first from a distance, then from bases ashore; and fourth, when surface forces would act alone. Clearly the Japanese high command had chosen the third option for their unsuccessful defense of the Marianas in June, when they attempted to "shuttle-bomb" our carriers using bases on Saipan, Tinian, and Guam to extend the range of their carrier planes beyond ours.

The document fell into Navy hands too late, of course, to be of use to Admiral Spruance and his Fifth Fleet forces invading the Marianas. And when it arrived on *New Jersey,* Halsey and Carney saw it, but what caught their interest was the heavy emphasis, spread over page after page, on the enemy's elaborate plans for shore-based air counterattacks. That, after all, was what we had just experienced as the Japanese threw wave after wave of shore-based aircraft at us when Third Fleet raided Okinawa and Formosa at the very gates of the Japanese homeland.

But Harris Cox's analysis of the captured document took a different direction. He had not been one of the Third Fleet senior staffers who had sailed as observers with Spruance in the June seafight, and hence was not as impressed by the "shuttle-bombing" tactic as Carney and Moulton, who were. And he was not an ACI officer, as Lawrence, Marshall, and I were— and thus concerned before all with ship- and shore-based air.

Harris had been schooled instead as one of the Office of Naval Intelligence reservists assigned to our surface ships—and it was the role the enemy's big surface ships, the Main Body in Navy parlance, might be expected to play that weighed on Harris's mind. He kept the document in our quarters and was forever pulling it out of a drawer and talking with me about it. He also went over it with Captain Cheek, our chief.

There could be no doubt that the Japanese were hitting us with all the shore-based air they could—all, that is, that they could assemble after losing so many planes in the big assault on our Third Fleet off Formosa. And now they had hurled their carrier-based air into the battle, too. At the same time, all of us in Flag Plot could see some sort of a coordinated move in the simultaneous advance of their heavy ships toward Surigao

Capt. Mike Cheek, intelligence chief (*left*), confers with Lt. Harris Cox, the author's roommate. It was Cox who studied the Japanese Z-plan and tried on October 24, 1944, to warn his superiors that in rushing north after the carriers, Halsey was doing exactly what the Japanese wanted him to do.

Strait at the south and San Bernardino Strait to the north of our Leyte beachhead.

According to the strategy laid down in the Z-Plan, the pattern in the developing Japanese moves was clearly discernible, said Harris. "Bear in mind," the document stated, "that the main objectives which must be destroyed are [the enemy's] transport convoys. Surface forces will make the transport convoy their primary objective, and will deliver a sudden attack." On the other hand, "the carrier nucleus will try as far as possible to operate outside the limits of the area [and] attack the enemy striking force on the flank."

And now, Harris said, the Japanese carrier force had done exactly that, maneuvering beyond the limit of our reconnaissance and then hitting us on our northern flank. The highest of all enemy priorities, as Harris read the document, was for the big surface ships to force their way into Leyte Gulf and spread destruction on the beachhead crammed with transports and debarking troops.

After watching the surface ships converge on Leyte from south and north, and after going over once more the overriding priority assigned to their mission, I too could suddenly divine that the Japanese were exposing, even expending their carriers in a desperate effort to draw us away so that the Main Body could get through San Bernardino Strait and attack MacArthur's invasion forces.

What to do? Orders were already going out. While I waited, Harris went up to present our case to Captain Cheek.

Our chief had already had something of a run-in with Air Officer Doug Moulton earlier in the evening when the searchers sent out by our night-operations carrier *Independence* found the Japanese surface force, now under cover of darkness, advancing once more toward San Bernardino Strait. Bill McMillan, assistant operations officer, later described to me what he termed a "furious" argument. In Flag Plot as assistant duty officer, the ordinarily taciturn Cheek tangled with Moulton, principal officer on duty. "They're coming through, I know," said Mike. "I've played poker with them in Tokyo." That was, for Mike Cheek, an outburst. He had never let on to any of us that he'd ever been in Japan.

But Moulton brushed off his argument that Third Fleet must not leave the strait unguarded. Orders had already gone out, Moulton said.

Now, the hour already nearing 2200, Cheek agreed to take our plea that Halsey was doing just what the Japanese hoped he would to higher authority, to Admiral Carney. Cheek himself had recognized the completion of the enemy's coordinated moves with the belated appearance of the carriers — but had not necessarily concluded that the carriers were decoys.

Cheek, alas, was not a strong voice. He had never had such close ties with Halsey as Col. Julian Brown, his predecessor as chief intelligence officer in the South Pacific. Brown had shared quarters as well as confidences with the admiral in Noumea. Cheek, who moved up when Brown for medical reasons had to return to the States, never enjoyed the same intimacy. An Annapolis man, he had been recalled as a reservist when the war broke out in the Far East. He was one of the most phlegmatic men I've ever known. It took our being caught in a great typhoon to draw from him the remark that he'd served on a destroyer that rolled 89 degrees and recovered in the North Atlantic in World War I. I never knew until long afterward that he'd won the Navy Cross for intelligence service before the Navy flew him out on one of the last planes from the Philippines in 1942. It was his way as intelligence officer on *New Jersey* to submit little notes to the chief of staff, who might or might not pass them on to Halsey. So no, Cheek was not a strong voice. He could not stand up to the flyboys. He came back saying he had presented our case to Admiral Carney. He told us Carney said Halsey was asleep, not to be disturbed.

Meanwhile *Independence* reported that its night searchers shadowed the enemy force "until it reached the southern tip of

Burias island and started northeastward between Burias and Ticao islands, when they were recalled." When Admiral Bogan, commanding TG 38.2, had gone on TBS to pass along this word, the voice from Third Fleet, presumably Moulton's, replied, "Yes, yes, we have that information." Years later the Avenger pilot, Lt. Bill Phelps, told me he watched the warships shine their searchlights at the steep shores as they steered in column through the narrow waters toward San Bernardino Strait. By the time his plane landed aboard at 2344, *Independence* was rushing north with the rest of us, leaving the strait unguarded.

10

SLAUGHTER AT SURIGAO

OUR IRREVERENT NAVY MEN, POKING FUN AT HIS GOD-like propensities, sometimes jeered that MacArthur thought he could walk on water. In the early days in the South Pacific they sang

> Oh they sent for the Army
> To come to Tulagi
> But General MacArthur said no.
> He gave as his reason
> This isn't the season
> And Tulagi has no U.S.O.

On their side of the Pope's Line, battling through the Solomons with no help from MacArthur, Navy men slanged him as "Dugout Doug" and jeered his grandiloquence with doggerel ending with the general ascending to heaven and announcing, "Move over, Lord, it's Mac." They mocked his godlike propensities when, as they said, he adopted the island-hopping tactic they had invented and perforce had to ask the Navy for help.

He couldn't walk on water after all.

To return to the Philippines, MacArthur needed seagoing help aplenty—and not just an amphibious fleet to put him and his 80,000 invasion troops ashore. Among the 600 ships the Navy supplied were a whole panoply of supporting warships—old battleships, cruisers, and destroyers needed for bombardment and fire support at the landing. And then, when on A day—plus four it became apparent that the Japanese navy was bent on counterattacking his beachhead, these warships were called into action.

With a two-prong advance on the Leyte beachhead looming, Third Fleet could strike the big force of heavy ships moving toward San Bernardino Strait. But after his carrier scouts found and attacked the smaller formation advancing toward Surigao Strait, Halsey left it for MacArthur's Navy, Seventh Fleet, to deal with. Throughout the day of October 24 MacArthur's Navy man, Admiral Kinkaid, methodically massed his forces to meet and smash the oncoming force, identified by our carrier pilots as two battleships, a heavy cruiser, and four destroyers.

By midmorning Kinkaid knew this was his challenge. At noon he alerted his ships to prepare for a night engagement. A destroyer screen was thrown around the transports in the harbor. The sixteen baby flattops flying close support to troops ashore redoubled their patrols against possible coordinated air attacks. And at 1443 Admiral Kinkaid ordered Adm. Jesse Oldendorf, Commander Bombardment and Fire Support Group, to meet and destroy the enemy warships advancing on Surigao.

It was an imposing and overpowering force that Kinkaid and Oldendorf assembled to meet the seven warships—six battleships, eight cruisers, and thirty-two destroyers, plus forty-five motor torpedo boats that were to patrol the approaches to the strait and provide early warning. The pace of the enemy's two-prong advance suggested they were aiming for a rendezvous in Leyte Gulf at dawn. So, as Oldendorf schemed it, his ships would meet and annihilate the enemy force as it threaded the strait—which was no more than 15 miles wide.

Across the end nearest the beachhead would be ranged his six old battleships, refloated and refurbished after Pearl Harbor. These ships with their big guns would sail slowly back and forth in Battle Line.

Forward of the battlewagons, the cruisers with their shorter-range guns would take station on each flank, Oldendorf himself in the heavy cruiser *Louisville* with the group on the left. And still further forward his thirty-two destroyers would be poised on each side of the strait to dart out at the oncoming Japanese as they filed up the channel and launch spread after spread of torpedoes. It was an overwhelming array, and Oldendorf's one concern as he met beforehand with Adm. Robert Hayler, Commander Battle Line, was that the supply of the big ships' armor-piercing shells as compared to bombardment ammunition was somewhat limited. Oldendorf knew that he had a big edge, but as he said afterward, "Never give a sucker an even break. If my opponent is foolish enough to come at me with an inferior force, I'm certainly not going to give him an even break." Taking no chances, he was careful to deploy his ships clear of Hibuson, the one small island in the strait. He remembered how Japanese warships had struck from behind Savo Island to surprise and sink three U.S. cruisers in an earlier night fight off Guadalcanal.

It was a dark, still night and the moon was up at 2236 when the first PTs tangled with the enemy some 30 miles short of the strait. Destroyers caught the speeding boats in their searchlights and fired. Shells straddled the PTs. One shell went right through PT-130, and PT-152, illuminated, took a 4.7-inch shell. Not until 0052 were their skippers able to get this contact report through to Oldendorf. He was glad to get it, the first sighting of the seven-ship formation since Third Fleet planes' attack on them at 0945 that morning. More PTs pestered the Japanese as they made their way into the strait. All told, thirty PTs got into action. They fired thirty-three torpedoes; all but one missed.

As the Japanese plodded on, it became the destroyers' turn. Eleven miles to the north Capt. Jesse Coward of Destroyer Squadron Ten already had the enemy on radar. At 0225 he warned PTs to get out of the way because his six greyhounds were coming down the strait. And down they swept at 45 knots, one trio close to the Leyte shore to keep out of enemy radar, the other rushing straight for the target.

It was the opening shot of the war's biggest destroyer attack. This first move was executed in silence, of course, because the first shot fired would give their presence away. At 0258 they sighted the target ships. At 0300 they launched fifteen torpedoes, range 8,200 to 9,300 yards. The Japanese were not surprised. As the greyhounds turned away they came under battleship and destroyer fire. Searchlights flashed, star shells burst overhead, 4.7-inch shells rained all around them. But spreading smoke as they withdrew, they escaped unhit and, zigzagging away, they listened impatiently — torpedoes run at about 35 MPH — for explosions. For whatever reason the Japanese ships did not turn and between 0308 and 0309 Coward's men heard explosions and saw one of the battleships veer out to the right. This early hit, which is credited to the destroyer *Melvin,* knocked one of the enemy's two capital ships out of the fight. Twenty minutes later the huge warship blew apart, bow and stern continuing to burn in separate pieces.

Cdr. Richard Phillips, leading the other three attackers, threw the next punch. Flashing out of the covering Leyte shore to the west, his column went to 30 knots and from as close as 7,500 yards let fly twenty-seven torpedoes. *Remey* was caught in a searchlight, but again the destroyers escaped behind smoke. And this time the Japanese, firing fiercely, evaded. They made two hard right turns which, as fate would have it, brought them squarely into the path of the attackers' torpedoes. Three enemy destroyers took torpedo hits. These have been credited to *McDermott.* Another hit the battleship leading the formation but did not stop her. This hit was credited to *Monssen.*

The first forty-five torpedoes had hit five of the seven target ships, and now destroyer attacks came thick and fast. Ten minutes later destroyers attacked from the right flank and launched at 0319 in the glare of a Japanese destroyer blowing up. Still others launched at 0323; one claimed a hit on the lead battle-

ship, which again did not stop. At 0349, just as they were ordered to retire, *Hutchins* fired off a spread of five fish, and saw
one hit and sink a destroyer. Last of all to attack was Capt. Ro-
land Smoot's Squadron 56, which had been screening left-flank
cruisers. All were taken under fire by the lead battleship's secondary battery, launched, missed, and sped away under smoke.
But the last to launch ran into punishing gunfire, and *Albert W.
Grant* was hit at 0407. This was a case of pressing luck a shade
too far. The cruisers and battleships, waiting for the enemy to
come within range, now at last opened up. At 0323 the Battle
Line, steaming slowly back and forth at the top of the strait,
had the enemy on their screens.

Admiral Hayler gave the signal to fire, and at 0353 *West
Virginia,* equipped with the latest fire-control radar, got off
the first 16-inch salvo, and soon had fired ninety-three rounds.
Then *Tennessee* and *California* joined in, firing 14-inch shells.
The Americans had achieved a seafighter's dream: they had
crossed the enemy's T, all right. But the other three battlewagons hardly got in on the carnage: *Maryland* got off six
salvos, *Mississippi* one, and *Pennsylvania* none at all.

At 0351 the eight cruisers began shooting — range about
8½ miles — and they really poured it on. *Columbia* was firing a
salvo every 12 seconds. All told they got off 3,100 rounds in 18
minutes.

For seven minutes of this hail of lethal projectiles the Japanese battleship plowed on, and even returned the cruisers' fire.
"The arched line of tracers in the darkness looked like a con-
tinual stream of lighted railroad cars going over a hill," said
Captain Smoot afterwards. Then at 0409 Admiral Oldendorf
called, "Cease fire." Word had reached him that *Grant,* making
its last torpedo attack, was being hit by friendly fire from a light
cruiser, later found to be *Denver,* and he wanted to give the
stricken destroyer time to get away.

In all *Grant* took eighteen hits, eleven of them six-inch shells
from *Denver. Newcomb,* turning just before *Grant,* scored yet

another torpedo hit on the Japanese battleship. *Newcomb* was ordered to tie up to *Grant* and haul the ship with its thirty-four dead and ninety-four wounded to safety.

When Oldendorf at 0419 ordered all ships to resume fire, none did. No targets were left within gun range. At that very moment the lead Japanese battleship, hit by innumerable shells from our battleships and cruisers, capsized and sank. Behind it the battered heavy cruiser, after taking more hits, was retiring and so was the one destroyer that had escaped serious damage. And now, just as Oldendorf was poised to order pursuit, something mystifying happened.

Unbeknownst to us at the time—although it was not hard to trace its passage afterward through scattered sightings and contacts along the way—an entirely different enemy force had arrived on the scene. At 0433 Admiral Hayler informed Oldendorf that he had three enemy ships on his screen. One was the retreating cruiser. The others were warships of the same Striking Force that had been sent south from Japan a fortnight earlier on the vain mission to finish off Third Fleet "remnants" off Formosa. Instead of returning to Japan, these ships had remained in the Formosa area and now had been dispatched south to beef up the force trying to penetrate Surigao.

Passing close to Panaon Island on their way in, they too had run afoul of the PTs. PT-132 got off the only torpedo to hit an enemy ship that night. His fish caught a light cruiser amidships and forced the ship to drop out of the formation. Stepping up speed to 26 knots, the other six ships charged into the strait just in time to see the Japanese battleships on fire and sinking.

They decided to withdraw. Their only contribution to the battle, apart from scrimmaging with PTs, were torpedoes launched as they turned back—torpedoes that hit nothing and came to rest harmlessly on the shores of Hibuson Island. And as they turned back, one of these ships crashed into the retreating heavy cruiser of the first force, suffering some damage.

Oldendorf's cruisers followed, pouring shells into the

wounded heavy cruiser until it was "burning like a city block." It lagged behind the newly arrived force, which got clean away except for the light cruiser left behind after PT-132's torpedo hit. In the final mop-up Oldendorf's flagship *Louisville* finished off parts of the first battleship that were still afloat at 0531, and his destroyers sank a last crippled destroyer at 0721. A few hours later planes from Kinkaid's jeep carriers found and bombed the much battered heavy cruiser, forcing the Japanese to scuttle it.

Thus ended the battle of Surigao Strait. It was a resounding victory, but not quite annihilation. As we soon learned, the second force of seven ships sent to follow and reinforce the bid for breakthrough entered Surigao Strait that night only to turn tail and make a getaway.

In Flag Plot on *New Jersey,* this was the outcome we expected — the six old battleships, five of them refloated after being sunk at Pearl Harbor, alone far outgunned the attackers, and what a barrage Oldendorf's warships laid down: 141 16-inch shells, 141 14-inchers, 4,281 six- and eight-inch shells, uncounted five-inchers, 148 torpedoes fired by destroyers, and 30 more fired by PTs. And on our side, just one destroyer damaged, ten PTs hit but only one sunk. Casualties: 37 killed, 114 wounded.

11

JEEP CARRIERS SAVE THE DAY

SIXTEEN BABY FLATTOPS CRUISED THAT SAME OCTOBER 25 dawn off Leyte-Samar. Makeshift carriers, they were built on merchant-ship hulls, and they were slow—top speed 17 knots or so. They were called escort carriers because they were first used to accompany convoys across the North Atlantic, and their pilots were trained to search out and destroy German U-boats. Here these auxiliary carriers were to launch planes to fly close cover for MacArthur's troops on Leyte.

Operating close offshore, each carrier deployed from fifteen to sixteen fighter planes, mostly Grumman Wildcats, and eight to twelve bombers, Martin Marauders, and some Grumman Avengers. Admiral Kinkaid, commanding Seventh Fleet, stationed these little carriers in three groups, each with a few screening destroyers or destroyer-escorts, about 30 miles apart —one group to the south, one in the middle, and one to the north off Samar Island. At dawn on October 24 all of them had already executed assigned tasks—one to launch the morning CAP over the transport-filled Leyte Gulf, another to drop supplies to a forward infantry post. At 0545 the southernmost group sent off a twenty-six-plane strike to attack the crippled warships trying to escape after the previous night's near-annihilation of the enemy force that sought to penetrate Surigao Strait.

But none of the three had launched any searches northward,

so it was Ens. Hans Jensen, flying his Avenger at 0640 on routine antisubmarine patrol, who first saw the unthinkable happening, the terrifying surprise—a surface force bearing down on a carrier force, a major enemy fleet capable of vastly superior speed and fire closing on a force of slow jeep flattops. The carrier force was Adm. Clifton Sprague's northernmost group of six baby flattops, and the surface force was none other than the main Japanese Striking Force that Halsey thought was routed. Far from it, this powerful force had transited the San Bernardino Strait in the night and, rounding Samar, were now in sight and already shooting.

Moments after Ensign Jensen stumbled onto the enemy armada, lookouts on Sprague's flagship *Fanshaw Bay* saw the flashes of guns firing at his plane. At 0658 the Japanese opened fire on the carrier force at 17 miles range. Admiral Sprague sized up the situation fast. The big warships with their pagoda-like masts were already shooting at his ships. Splashes were landing just astern of his force. He ordered speed 16 knots, soon increased to 17½, flank speed to eastward. Within 10 minutes every available plane was launched. But the chase was on, and he never got the chance to turn into the wind to recover planes.

At 0700 he sent off a dispatch notifying admirals Kinkaid and Halsey that he was under attack by surface ships. But even the most urgent messages took time to get through. On his command ship in Leyte Gulf Kinkaid received the shocking report soon enough. The first word to reach Halsey was a 0707 flash in plain language from Kinkaid that Clifton Sprague's jeep-carrier force was being shelled by warships off Samar.

This message arrived in Flag Plot at 0822 and caused a mighty stir, not least at the intelligence desk. But at that distance Halsey couldn't do a thing to save the little carriers from their pursuers, and at that particular moment he could not let go—he was leading Third Fleet's Battle Line after an all-night charge to the north and was now so near the target carriers he could taste their blood. But there was one thing that he could do. At 0830 he summoned his ultimate reserve, ordering his fourth fast-carrier group, already recalled from Ulithi to fuel in mid-ocean and join the assault on the Japanese carriers, to break off fueling and rush to launch a long-distance strike at the surface ships as soon as possible. But TG 38.1's planes couldn't possibly get there before afternoon, by which time the powerful Japanese fleet would have brushed aside the jeep carriers and entered Leyte Gulf.

Or so it seemed.

Clifton Sprague and his men were fighting for their lives. In what stretched into a wild, 2½-hour running fight, the first few minutes were the most desperate. It should have been a chase to swift death, but it wasn't. The Japanese should have overtaken the trudging carriers, but they didn't. The big guns of the enemy force, including the world's biggest mounted on their superbattleship, should have knocked out all the American ships, but they didn't.

Perhaps the Japanese were as nonplussed as the Americans at this strange encounter. Certainly some of their tactics helped the defenders. For some reason, as if desirous of holding the weather gauge, the Japanese formation kept on a southeasterly course after Sprague, hoping for help from Leyte Gulf, turned south and then southwest. For another, instead of keeping a tight formation the warships operated individually. And because they advanced with no air cover, the fact that it was now broad daylight meant that if the little carriers could only gain time, their planes could attack the enemy ships.

And attack they did, though at first only in twos and threes. *Kitkun Bay* managed to launch eleven fighters and six Avengers at 0700. Their leader, Cdr. R. L. Fowler, stayed aloft all day and at the most desperate hour, when the enemy cruisers closed, firing eight-inch salvos on the port flank, began to organize coordinated counterattacks.

But first Clifton Sprague had somehow to stay ahead of the advancing Japanese. All six of his carriers fired so many rounds from their single five-inchers that they soon ran short of ammunition. The same was true of the first counterattacking planes: having expended their bombs and torpedoes, they were reduced to making dummy runs against the nearest cruisers. At least for the first five or six minutes the Japanese shells were not hitting. *Fanshaw Bay* and *White Plains* on the exposed flank had close calls. *White Plains* took three 14-inch straddles by 0704. The third salvo twisted the vessel violently, throwing men off their feet, tossing gear about and opening the generator circuit-breakers so that momentarily steering control was lost. Colored geysers sprouted all around; the projectiles were loaded with dye—yellow, purple, pink. "They're shooting at us in Technicolor," cried a sailor on *White Plains*. At that moment, Admiral Sprague said later, "the volume and accuracy of the fire was increasing, and it did not appear that any of our ships could survive another five minutes."

Just then his ships ran under a providential rain squall, which gave them 15 minutes' cover. It was then, "in the ultimate circumstances," that he called upon his destroyers to launch a torpedo counterattack. "Small boys . . . intercept" was his command. This surely was a desperate move, for it meant charging into the teeth of the oncoming enemy. They were just six in number, and two were the smaller destroyer-escorts. But even before emerging from the rain squall the 2,000-ton *Johnston*, nearest the enemy, turned and raced toward the foe with a gallantry that courted certain death, pumping out 200 rounds in rapid-fire salvos throughout the charge. Then, at 10,000 yards Cdr. Ernest E. Evans, the fighting Cherokee skipper, let fly with all his ten torpedoes, turned, and began to retire under heavy smoke. Japanese guns shortly snuffed out *Johnston*'s life but not before a surviving officer heard underwater explosions at the right time on the target heavy cruiser. *Hoel, Heermann,* and two destroyer-escorts made their breakneck dashes, launched torpedoes—and *Hoel* and *Samuel B. Roberts* also went down under point-blank shellfire. But their smoke screened the fleeing carriers and their torpedoes forced the enemy ships to turn away to evade. The superbattleship in the rear, with its fearsome 18.1-inch guns, lost so much distance that it fell out of the fight.

The leading Japanese cruisers kept inching up on the flank, and their heaviest shellfire fell on the carriers furthest back. *Gambier Bay,* most exposed of all, was hit at 0820, immediately fell astern, and was lost—riddled by cruiser projectiles fired at 2,000-yard range. Sprague's ship *Fanshaw Bay* took four eight-inch hits and two near-misses. *White Plains,* straddled by a six-inch salvo, suffered damage. *Kitkun Bay,* though never hit, took some casualties from near-miss shell fragments. *Kalinin Bay,* rocked by thirteen eight-inch hits, managed to keep going on one engine—and, said Sprague later, by "the heroic efforts of her crew. Bos'n's crews wrested under five feet of water to plug up big holes in the hull; engineers waded knee-deep in oil, choking in the stench of burned rubber; quartermasters steered the ship for hours from an emergency wheel below, as fire scorched the deck on which they stood." Damage would have been far greater if the Japanese warships had not used only SAP (semi-armor-piercing) shells, so that again and again the projectiles passed right through the thin-skinned carriers without exploding. And when the enemy destroyers delivered their torpedo attack, they launched from so far away that their torpedoes broached before reaching their targets.

Meanwhile, even during the rain squall, all six carriers had launched every available plane. At first the planes attacked in sheer desperation. They bored in with torpedoes and bombs, and when these were expended they made dummy runs. Lt. Paul Garrison, flying a Wildcat, made twenty strafing runs, ten of them dry. Commander Fowler coached five *Kitkun Bay* planes to dive through the clouds in a first attack. He then saw two battleships heading toward the middle carrier group 30 miles to the south and flashed a warning to Adm. Felix Stump commanding that group as 14-inch splashes started falling astern of his destroyers.

And now planes from the other jeep carrier groups joined the counterattack. It happened that Kinkaid, preparing for the enemy approach to Surigao, had ordered all escort carriers to be prepared to arm Avengers with torpedoes and Wildcats with bombs. One of these attackers drew first blood, hitting and slowing a heavy cruiser. With Commander Fowler's guidance from overhead, at 0830 a half dozen torpedo planes and twenty fighters were able to deliver the first coordinated attack. Soon after Fowler mustered another:

> We circled the heavy cruisers for three turns to gain a cirrus cloud cover and attacked from out of the sun and through this cloud at about 0905. We caught the second heavy cruiser (*Mogami* class) in the column completely by surprise as we received absolutely no anti-aircraft fire. At this time we had only four torpedo-bombers as the twelve fighters and the other torpedo-bombers had fallen out of formation in the thick weather. We completed all dives in about 35 seconds, scoring five hits amidships on the stack, one hit and two near-misses on the stern and three hits on the bow. The third plane hitting the stern sent the heavy cruiser into a sharp right turn. After pulling out of the dive, I observed the heavy cruiser to go ahead about 500 yards, blow up and sink within five minutes.

On *Fanshaw Bay* Admiral Sprague was engaged in dodging Japanese destroyers' torpedoes when he heard a signalman yell, "Goddamit, boys, they're getting away." "I could not believe my eyes, but it looked as if the whole Japanese fleet was retiring," the admiral said later. "It took a whole series of reports from circling planes to convince me. And still I could not get the fact to soak into my battle-numbed brain. At best I had expected to be swimming by this time."

But once again the unbelievable had happened. For whatever reason—and by now the enemy had lost two big cruisers—the powerful formation that had pounced on the seem-

ingly defenseless force ceased fire and turned away. But what
was still more puzzling, they stayed in the offing. At 1100 Clifton Sprague reported that they appeared to be reforming. Kinkaid, on his command ship in Leyte harbor, thought to call the
exhausted victors of the Surigao night action into the gulf to
stave off the invaders. But the Striking Force did not return to
attack.

Instead, they circled uncertainly, thereby giving the planes
from the escort carriers plenty of chance to keep hammering
them. By now Clifton Sprague's battered force was getting lots
of help from the carrier planes of the other two groups. The
southernmost group, which first had to recover planes from the
dawn strike launched against the Surigao stragglers, mounted
four attacks—one in an immediate scramble, a second at 1115,
a third a well-coordinated fighter-torpedo plane attack, and a
final thrust at 1700. Admiral Stump's middle group delivered
six strikes—at 0745, 0844, 0935, 1145, 1330, and 1420. The first
claimed two torpedo hits on the two cruisers closest to catching
Clifton Sprague's carriers. Few of the big enemy ships escaped
damage, and three in all went under.

The dauntless Commander Fowler, having directed the
morning strikes, landed on *Manila Bay* in Admiral Stump's formation, refueled, and took off again at 1100 to lead some thirty-
five torpedo planes and thirty fighters northward and found the
enemy still circling indecisively. The Wildcats strafed ahead of
the diving Avengers, which this time carried four 500-pound
SAP bombs. One bomb went right through a battleship's bow
and exploded in the water. Another made what Fowler called a
sure hit on a heavy cruiser.

This was the moment when the enemy turned and ran for
San Bernardino Strait. But more *Kitkun Bay* planes attacked
an already damaged heavy cruiser at 1300, and Commander
Fowler watched it sink at 1322. And the 100-plane strike that
Halsey had ordered to the rescue arrived from the decks of
TG 38.1's fast carriers. This was one of the longest carrier strikes

of the Pacific war—335 miles—and the planes had to carry bombs instead of the heavier torpedoes. The first planes struck at 1315, and another forty-seven planes attacked right afterward. They claimed many hits but none could be confirmed. They lost ten planes at the target, four planes that ran out of gas and ditched, three others landed on the jeep carriers, and a number crash-landed on the Tacloban strip. At great risk and considerable cost, this attack out of the northeast unquestionably quickened the enemy resolve to get out before more fast-carrier planes appeared on the scene.

But it was the torpedo planes from the little jeep carriers that routed the enemy Striking Force and saved all those defenseless troops on the landing ships in Leyte Gulf from their 16-inch—18.1-inch!—guns. Already at 1300 the enemy had turned tail and headed for San Bernardino Strait.

12

THE KAMIKAZES

JAPAN'S SHORE-BASED AIR WAS SUPPOSED TO HAVE ALL THE
advantages when pitted against our fast but extremely vulnerable carrier forces. But it hadn't turned out that way. In the epic
three-day set-to off Formosa, Halsey's slashing attackers routed
the Japanese defenders over their island airfields, caught and
smashed their drawn-up airplanes on the ground by the hundreds, and then, when the bombers were brought in from Japan
to demolish us with their deadly torpedoes, shot them down
without damage to a single aircraft carrier. Massed attacks by
Halsey's carrier airmen worked over every airfield in the Philippines until it was the Americans, not the Japanese, who held
command of the air over the islands on invasion day. If Japanese shore-based air, rushed in from north, south, and even the
Asian mainland, thought to strike us so hard that their surface
fleet could penetrate and annihilate our beachhead, they had
failed utterly in their mission.

It is now known that even before this rout of their navy's
best air units, the Japanese leadership, after the string of defeats
culminating in the loss of the Marianas in June, began organiz-
ing suicide formations on a large scale. Their pilots were now
ill-trained, their planes inferior to the Americans'. When sent
into combat they were apt to be shot down before they could
bring down an American plane or damage an American ship.
And after the defeat at Formosa, the Japanese were desperate.

In a last-ditch effort the top Japanese air commander felt compelled to abandon his Manila headquarters and pay a frantic visit to front-line bases in eastern Luzon. There he called in person upon pilots in certain units to fly out to suicide-bomb American carriers that could be stopped in no other way. We knew nothing, of course, of his crazy decision, although in Third Fleet staff we commonly spoke of desperate Japanese air assaults as "suicidal."

On October 25, however, on this third day of the Battle of Leyte, our fast carriers were out of range to the northeast. And so it was that the first Kamikazes fell upon the same hard-pressed jeep carriers that were trying valiantly to stave off the big warships off Samar.

"Kamikaze" is a word that's become part of our language. It means "Divine Wind"—and recalls an earlier hour when Japan was in peril, the typhoon-like storm that blew up in 1570 and miraculously shattered a Chinese fleet on its way to conquer Japan. As conceived now by the desperate commander, it summoned young airmen to be modern *samurais,* to fly against the foe with no intent to return. That was the unique call: to attack with no thought of ever coming back.

The first Special Attack Corps at Malabacan comprised twenty-six young fighter pilots. The high commander who recruited them said this offered death with the highest honor. For each "human missile" a wingman would bear witness of his crash-dive so that his warrior's proud end could be reported back to the emperor. The fliers, all aged 18 to 20 or so, readily volunteered. As one young pilot wrote before his final sortie:

> We were bubbling with eagerness. Shinkei and I swore to each other that we would sink the largest ships we could find. I thought of my age, nineteen, and of the saying: "To die while people still lament your death, to die while you are pure and fresh, this is truly Bushido." Yes, I was following the way of the samurai.

In that spirit Yamahiro Saito, a university student, wrote, "I will end my story at 21 years. I give these words to my father. Ride the sky! I am the shield of the Emperor as I ride." In that spirit Masahito Uyamura wrote his four-year-old daughter, "Grow up and be a healthy and big girl. Daddy will make an attack on the enemy. When you grow up you will understand." In that spirit, hearing of a U.S. carrier force east of Leyte, the first twenty took off from Luzon on the morning of October 20—they ran into bad weather and had to turn back. In that spirit, Lt. Yoshiyasu Kuno headed east from Cebu late the next day but was never heard from again. And it was in that spirit that members of the Shikishima unit flew out from Malabacan on the morning of October 25.

And so fate decreed that this "mission with no return," this samurai quest for "the largest ships we could find," happened upon the very baby flattops already running for their lives before the guns of the big Japanese warships.

This was too much.

It was just as the shelling broke off and Admiral Sprague's flattops at last had a chance to land a few planes that five Kamikaze fighters, escorted by four other Zekes, sighted the jeep carriers. Lt. Yuko Seki, with one bomb under each wing, peeled off at about 3,000 feet and made a run at *St. Lo* from starboard. Gunners on the carrier's starboard side fired furiously but the plane still came on. Sweeping down at no more than 50 feet above the deck, the suicider turned sharp right and hit *St. Lo*'s flight deck at about the No. 5 restraining wire, and a little to the port side. There was a tremendous explosion and flash as one or both bombs went off, ripping a big hole in the deck. What was left of the plane skidded over the bow, scattering fragments across the deck, and plunged into the sea.

St. Lo was doomed. Smoke poured up from the hole and out the sides from the hangar deck. Although hoses were run out at once, within a minute or so another huge explosion burst on the hangar deck, followed by an even bigger blast that rolled back part of the flight deck, then a still bigger explosion that tore out more of the flight deck and blew the forward elevator out of its shaft. Captain McKenna ordered abandon ship, and *St. Lo* sank at 1125. At great risk Adm. Clifton Sprague detached every surviving ship from his antisubmarine screen, and the four, working until 1534, took aboard some 400 survivors.

The Kamikazes went after three others of Clifton Sprague's already battered carriers. Slightly before the *St. Lo* attack another Zeke death-dived on *Kitkun Bay*. This suicider missed the bridge, passed over the island, and crashed on the port catwalk before bouncing into the sea. But the bomb he carried exploded, causing considerable damage. Two others went after *Fanshaw Bay* but both were shot down. Still another dived on *White Plains,* and gunners could see their tracers blazing into the fuselage and wing roots as the plane roared down. No more than a few yards astern, the plane rolled over and plunged, missing the catwalk by inches and exploding between that level and the water. *White Plains* shook off the blast and kept station. In its action report, *White Plains* called these first Kamikazes "devil divers."

Actually, it was the southernmost of the three escort carrier groups that had the dubious distinction, a few hours earlier, of undergoing the very first deliberate Kamikaze attack of the war. At 0740 that same morning, as these four little flattops were recovering planes, six fighters from Davao in southern Mindanao jumped them. One took *Santee* by surprise. Diving out of a cloud so low-hanging that gunners had no time to fire a single shot, the plane crashed the flight deck on the port side forward and plunged on through the hangar deck. The crash left a hole, but no bomb explosion was felt, or *Santee* might have gone the way of *St. Lo*. Fires blazed, but fast work got them under control within 11 minutes. *Santee* lost sixteen dead, twenty-seven wounded, but kept going. Half a minute after this attack, another Kamikaze dived from astern at *Suwannee,* only to be hit by shipboard AA fire. The plane veered off toward *Sangamon*.

But a shell from *Suwannee*'s only five-incher caused the suicider to swerve and splash without having hit either target. A third Kamikaze dived on *Petrof Bay,* but was shot down by the ship's AA—a very near miss. *Suwannee,* having splashed two Zekes, spotted a third overhead at 5,000 feet. Hit by ship's gunfire and trailing smoke, this suicider plummeted almost straight down and hit *Suwannee* about 40 feet forward of the after elevator, making a 10-foot hole in the flight deck. The Kamikaze's bomb went off in the hangar deck, ripping both decks and knocking out the after plane elevator. By dint of speedy damage control, fires were put out, the flight deck temporarily patched, and takeoffs and landings resumed at 1009.

These blows—like the sinking of Third Fleet's light carrier *Princeton* the day before—failed to save the Japanese surface fleet from decisive damage inflicted by these same jeep carriers. But in their frustration at the inability of their land-based air to help their warships accomplish the destruction of MacArthur's invasion forces, they had ratcheted their defensive tactics to a new pitch of fanatical desperation. Kamikazes were something new, even in modern warfare. And what *White Plains* called their "devil diver tactics," employed by a formally constituted and constantly replenished Special Attack Corps, would henceforth be the chief form of air combat offered by an enemy fighting to the death in retreat.

These first Kamikaze attacks, together with difficulties in bringing up MacArthur's land-based air to the sodden airstrips on Leyte, forced a change in U.S. invasion plans. In their heroic stand on October 25 the jeep carriers had absorbed a lot of punishment—more than 2,000 casualties, most of them killed or missing, 130 planes lost, 5 ships sunk, and almost every surviving carrier out of ammunition and in need of repairs. They simply had to pull back to Manus, said Kinkaid.

And so it was that the Kamikazes caught up with Third Fleet. Told that the baby flattops would no longer be present to fly CAP over the Leyte beachhead, Halsey put aside his plans to withdraw Task Force 38 to Ulithi for rest and replenishment, and led TGs 38.2 and 38.4 forward to protect and support MacArthur's beachhead.

On the third day a suicide fighter found TG 38.2 and made a Kamikaze dive on the big carrier *Intrepid.* The plane struck a port gun platform and caromed into the sea—ten men died, six were wounded. The following day TG 38.4 ran into much more serious Kamikaze trouble. *Enterprise's* action report called it "one of the most vicious enemy attacks" this most battle-hardened of flattops "had ever encountered." This time the CAP, four fighters from *Belleau Wood* and six from *Enterprise,* failed to intercept, although CAP and attackers were seen to merge on the radar screen 40 miles out. Our planes failed to sight the bogey, presumably because the enemy was at 18,000 feet and just starting to glide.

Another division of CAP tallyhoed a second raid 60 miles out, shot down five Zekes, and drove the sixth away. But the first six enemy planes closed on TG 38.4 just as the formation was swinging to port and plummeted down out of the sun. Two dove on *Franklin.* The first struck just abaft the island structure, making a 40-foot hole in the flight deck and knocking out a plane elevator. Orange sheets of flame burst from the deck, and thirty-six planes were destroyed. Twenty minutes later gasoline fumes from ruptured belly tanks on the hangar deck exploded, and fierce fires burned for two hours. Fifty-six men were killed, fourteen seriously injured. The second plane, after dropping a bomb that near-missed *Franklin,* veered crazily under fire from *Enterprise's* port guns and lurched toward the light carrier *Belleau Wood.* Improbably this Kamikaze warrior—seen to be wearing a skintight yellow-and-green uniform—found his mark. The plane crashed through *Belleau Wood's* flight deck, destroying twelve planes that had been spotted for takeoff, and killed ninety-two crew besides fifty-four seriously wounded.

About eight minutes later, another plane plunged from high altitude toward *San Jacinto.* Under intense AA fire, this suicider plunged into the sea just off the carrier's port bow. The next plane started its dive for *Enterprise,* was hit repeatedly by 20-mm and 40-mm fire until it burst into flame, crossed the deck abaft the island no more than 10 feet above the heads of portside gun crews, and plunged into the sea less than 25 yards off the port quarter.

At 1433 two more Kamikazes dived at *San Jacinto.* The first came in from abaft starboard as the ship swung hard to port, missed the ship by feet only, and crashed off the bow, littering the flight deck and forecastle with debris of plane and pilot. The second plane, also hit by AA, missed so narrowly that debris and saltwater showered the full length of the ship.

At 1437 *San Jacinto*'s AA fire blew a wing off yet another plane making a suicide run at *Enterprise.* This Kamikaze crashed into the sea just short of his target. "We were fighting for our lives," said *Enterprise*'s action report afterward. Admiral Davison had to transfer his flag from the wounded *Franklin* to *Enterprise,* and damage to *Franklin* and *Belleau Wood* was so extensive that they retired to Ulithi under escort.

These were desperate hours — we all heard the reports numbly in Flag Plot. (We had of course witnessed the suicide crash on *Intrepid,* whose station in TG 38.2 was only 1,000 yards off the bow of Halsey's flagship *New Jersey.*) Now, as the Japanese sprang their last, impossible-to-believe weapon, all in Third Fleet knew as never before since the deadly night battles in the Solomons that shipboard personnel would catch it as surely as our pilots did. Too late, the Navy's ordnance men saw that the fleet's automatic AA weapons — the 40-mm and 50-cals that had served so well earlier — were simply too light and short-range to disable the Kamikazes before they crashed us. Before our side finally subdued them with an even more impossible-to-believe weapon, the A-bomb, Japanese suiciders flew 2,550 one-way missions, hit 74 of our ships, killed 12,300 of our shipboard officers and men, and wounded 36,400 others.

13

BULL'S RUN

IT WAS NOT UNTIL NEARLY MIDNIGHT, AFTER THE EMBAT-tled action of October 24, that Halsey could pull together the three fast-carrier groups and charge north after the only important element of the Japanese fleet not yet brought under attack. That force had been sighted too late to attack on the twenty-fourth, but if it was poised to strike a second time on the morrow Third Fleet had now marshaled an overwhelming force of sixty-four ships and was determined to get in the attack first.

Admiral Mitscher now resumed tactical command, but it was Halsey who called the shots. Both believed the Japanese could be taken by surprise, but when Third Fleet told the night carrier *Independence* to launch five night-searchers northward at midnight, Mitscher objected that the planes' radars would give our presence away. At 0029 Third Fleet told Mitscher by TBS, "Due to our commitment to the south, desire you launch search now."

That was a curious reason to give, committed as Halsey was to attacking the enemy carrier force. He said later he was concerned lest the enemy carriers slip past him and "have a free crack at [MacArthur's] transports." But at 0205 one of the searchers made radar contact with the carrier force—three large ships, three smaller ships, course 120, speed 15 knots. Thereupon Halsey ordered "Form Leo." "Leo" was Task Force 34.

And so in the dead of night, while *Independence* kept trying to verify its plotted position placing the enemy only 80 miles north of us, the six great battlewagons pulled out from their stations screening the carriers and took position in Battle Line 10 miles ahead of Task Force 38. Three thousand men on each of the big ships readied for action.

Excitement rose in Flag Plot. After reporting a second group of large enemy ships north of our onrushing battleships and their screening vessels, the tracking plane had to break off and return because of engine trouble. The relief plane also ran into difficulties, this time with its radar equipment. Thenceforth we were in the dark as we plowed northward.

Independence reported some doubt as to whether its pilot had correctly reported the position of the nearest force. But at 0313 Mitscher ordered all carriers to arm their first deck-load strikes immediately, to launch their strikes along with their dawn searches, and to have their attacking groups orbiting north of our force so as to get a big jump when the target ships were found. Meanwhile, Third Fleet, trying to make sense of conflicting contact reports, told Mitscher on TBS the enemy might be no more than 40 miles away, and Mitscher's staff replied, "We estimate enemy could be distance from 35 to 85 miles, do you concur?" Of two things all were sure: the gap was closing fast, and Task Force 34 was going to see action.

Dawn broke, October's bright blue weather, a day, we all thought, for dreadnoughts. On deck we watched the great ships surging forward in line abreast. *South Dakota* had broken out its battle flag — an enormous Stars and Stripes that stood gloriously straight out as Task Force 34 rushed ahead. In an hour or two, we thought, our battleships would start thundering at Japanese ships.

At 0648, as all our thoughts were riveted on the impending battle, a message arrived from Kinkaid. Sent at 0212, this dispatch from Seventh Fleet reported "our surface forces now engaging enemy forces" in Surigao Strait. In Third Fleet this mes-

sage could be greeted with satisfaction and even a certain con-
descension as we, the much more powerful force, having
(as our chiefs thought) turned back the larger threat to Mac-
Arthur's beachhead the day before, were now girding to finish
off the rest of the Imperial Japanese fleet. Appended to the message was the query, "Is Task Force 34 guarding San Bernardino
Strait?" And with almost a "Why do you ask?" air, Third Fleet
shot off this unruffled reply just seven minutes later: "Negative.
Task Force 34 is with carrier group now engaging enemy carrier
forces."

For the next hour a flurry of messages filled Flag Plot as
Third Fleet waited impatiently for the first flash report that the
target carriers had been located. Frustration mounted. The
cagey enemy had foxed us. Instead of continuing southward
and barging right into our clutches, they had turned away
in the night, apparently alerted by radar of our shadowing
snooper, and headed back north. So it took longer for our dawn
search to find them, and when they did the Japanese, in two
formations, turned out to be not 50 or 60 but a good 180 miles
away. Our deckload strikes, confidently launched at the same
time as our dawn searchers and ordered to orbit 40 miles north
of us to get the jump on the enemy, did not get in their attack
until an hour had gone by.

At 0803 we heard the shout over the air frequencies: "I have
the target in sight." At 0812: "The destroyers below are firing at
us"; and another voice: "One ship has just let go with his main
batteries." Finally, we judged, the attack was commencing.

At that moment the news reached us from the south. At
0822 Kinkaid's urgent 0707 dispatch was handed to Halsey:
"CTU 77.4.3 [Clifton Sprague with his escort carriers off Sa-
mar] reports enemy battleships and cruisers 15 miles astern unit
and firing on him. Position is 80 miles bearing 060 from No-
monhon island."

Reading this dispatch at our standup intelligence desk, I
knew at once that Mike Cheek had been everlastingly right the

night before in arguing that these very warships were coming through the strait. And even the unshakeable Doug Moulton knew it when a further message came through from Kinkaid: "Sprague under fire from enemy battleships cruisers—evidently came through San Bernardino strait during night." And two minutes later came the cry of calamity, in plain English: Send Lee! And "request immediate strike by fast carriers."

Halsey, who had never expected to hear of a carrier force overtaken by surface ships in this man's war, was pretty dashed, too. His face was ashen. But even when it was uncomfortably plain that the ships his planes had supposedly savaged the day before had covered a distance of 200 miles thereafter, he couldn't quite believe that these battered warships could shoot their way into Leyte Gulf. So he spurned the chance that if he detached his fast battleships right away, they might dash back south in time at least to cut off the Japanese if they should return through San Bernardino Strait. Send Lee? He had committed Lee's Task Force 34 to the attack. "Attack Repeat Attack" had been Halsey's message from Noumea to the carriers back in the dark days of 1942 when the Japanese threatened to force us out of Guadalcanal. And attack was his watchword now.

He was no longer committing his fast battleships to mere mopping up of enemy warships left crippled by our carrier-plane attacks. He now held that "when an opportunity presents itself to engage a major portion of the enemy fleet, every possible weapon should be brought to bear against the enemy. An advancing heavy surface force that can attack the enemy during the course of air strikes offers the best opportunity for the complete annihilation of the enemy force." This was what Halsey wrote after the battle. This was the admiral's thinking as he led the combined air and surface forces forward on the morning of October 25. John Marshall, in Flag Plot, noticed that the admiral sat silent on his transom. Suddenly, to no one in particular, but as if talking to himself, he muttered, "When I get my teeth into something, I hate to let go." Then he lapsed into silence, his jaw set like a bulldog's.

In response, however, to Seventh Fleet's plea for help, Halsey was ready to summon his ultimate reserve. Within minutes of Kinkaid's call, Third Fleet radioed new orders to his one uncommitted carrier group, and Moulton, the unshakeable Moulton of the night before, wrote the dispatch. It was addressed to Adm. John McCain, who already had orders to break off TG 38.1's retirement to Ulithi for rest and replenishment, refuel in mid-ocean, and join the onslaught on the Japanese carriers. At 0940, 10 minutes after receiving orders to "strike as practicable" northward, McCain got Halsey's new directive: break off fueling and rush toward Leyte, where "at best speed possible launch strike earliest possible" at the warships attacking the jeep carriers.

From *New Jersey*'s flag bridge we could see the resplendent sight of six battlewagons charging abreast into battle. And in Flag Plot we could now hear the shouts of the airmen as they pulled out of their bombing runs and looked back at the destruction they had wrought. At 0850 Mitscher could already tell Halsey by voice radio that two carriers had been hit and a third, a light carrier, already exploded and sunk.

While it is true that Third Fleet broke radio silence once at 0300 to report our night searcher's contact with enemy carriers only 100 miles north of us and to add cryptically, "Own force of three groups concentrated," news of what Halsey was up to was skimpy. Kinkaid wasn't the only one puzzled. At 1000 Nimitz, who never intervened in battle, saw the reports of surface ships shelling Seventh Fleet's escort carriers and sent Halsey a radio: "Where is Task Force 34?"

This fateful message arrived in Flag Communications Center three decks below Flag Plot at 1000. Lt. (jg) Bob Balfour decoded it as follows: "Where is rept where is Task Force 34 RR The world wonders." That last part was padding, added by an even more youthful communicator in Hawaii. And when Balfour handed the tape to his supervisor, Lt. Burt Goldstein, Goldstein knew at once that the last part was padding, separated clearly enough from the first part by "nulls." Yet the way it read Goldstein couldn't be sure that it wasn't part of the message. He tapped out the signal, "Important message coming up," and after getting an acknowledgment slipped it into the pneumatic tube.

In Flag Plot the usual communications officer was not present. Assistant Operations Officer Bill McMillan pulled out the tape, took one look at it, and handed it to Capt. Ham Dow, fleet communications officer who happened to be present. Dow handed it to Halsey, who was seated beside Carney on the leather transom he often occupied when in Flag Plot.

The admiral turned red. Furious at the rebuke, Halsey threw the tape on the floor and stamped on it shouting, "What right has Chester to send me a goddamn message like that?" He turned and went down the ladder to his quarters, followed by Carney. In Flag Plot there was silence—except for the yelps on air frequencies as Task Force 38 airmen slammed the Japanese carriers.

What passed between Halsey and Carney thereafter is not known—and judging from Carney's oral history recorded years later, never will be. But nearly an hour passed. Then at 1100 Carney emerged to hand Operations Officer Rollo Wilson this message: We're turning back. The dispatch ordered the major portion of Task Force 34, including all of Lee's Battle Line, to reverse course and steam south to help Kinkaid, although our plot chart showed that we could not get there before the next day. Halsey had no choice. Even without the derisory padding, Nimitz's query amounted to a reprimand. The Commander-in-Chief Pacific Fleet was alarmed for the safety of Seventh Fleet, and Halsey, having concentrated his fleet to annihilate the carrier force, was obliged to desist with the quarry almost within

range of his massed 16-inchers. He had to comply. Taking TG
38.2 along to give us air cover, we rushed right past the rest of
Task Force 38's carriers, bound *away* from the day's targets.

In Flag Plot we were still on tenterhooks. We feared yet more
calamitous news from the south as a consequence of our failure
to guard San Bernardino Strait. We were especially appalled
when at 1152 we intercepted another Kinkaid dispatch—this
time ordering destroyers well to the east of Leyte to break off
shepherding a troop convoy and dash to help hold off "enemy
in strength threatening to force entrance Leyte Gulf."

Our fears were not at all eased by the confusion. More Kinkaid signals kept coming in for Third Fleet, and apprehension
rose and fell like a yo-yo. One radio message, arriving first but
sent later, said, "Enemy returning to attack enemy carriers."
The prior message when it arrived brought only brief relief: "Situation looks better—enemy force now retiring to the
north-eastward." Half an hour later came a third dispatch: "My
situation has again become very serious—enemy fast battleships and heavy cruisers returning to attack my carrier groups
and threatening convoys." Much later we learned that it wasn't
just the communications that were confused: the Japanese admiral, evidently uncertain about our whereabouts, was mixed
up and couldn't make up his mind what to do.

By this time we started to hear the air frequency yelps from
the south. TG 38.1's airmen, guided to the target by a *Hornet*
search plane, were arriving to attack the Japanese warships.
McCain and his carriers had already performed prodigies to get
there. At 0900 the force had received Halsey's orders to break
off mid-ocean fueling. At 0930 Admiral Halsey's next message
ordered them to "strike as practicable" against the carriers.

Ten minutes later McCain got the countermanding orders
from Third Fleet to rush southward to the aid of Kinkaid.
McCain proceeded to bend on 30 knots. But he could see that
his planes would have to launch from so far away that they'd

probably have to land afterward at Tacloban—and he couldn't get an answer out of Leyte whether the Tacloban strip had yet been captured from the Japanese.

Not only that, his Avengers and Marauders would not be able to carry the heavier torpedoes such a long distance, so all torpedo planes had to be rearmed with bombs. And fighter planes had to be fitted with extra wing tanks. In a fantastic feat of scrambling, TG 38.1's five carriers launched deckload strikes at 1030.

It was this group of planes that struck the Japanese warriors at 1300. (Still another strike was launched later.) Flying with their bombloads to the extreme limit of their range, they claimed some damage. Many had to land in the water and on the captured but still unserviceable strip at Tacloban. Still, a 200-plane strike was warning enough, especially for a Japanese admiral who evidently had trouble making up his mind, to beat it before more arrived. But it was the torpedo planes from the little jeep carriers that saved the day. Already at 1300 the Japanese had turned tail and headed for San Bernardino.

Meanwhile, per Halsey's 1100 order, we in our vaunted battleships rushed south—*away* from the targets of the day. In the *New Jersey* there was only dejection. Third Fleet staff were crestfallen. John Marshall found Mike Cheek in his quarters. Cheek, his head in his hands, groaned, "And it could have been the greatest victory since Trafalgar." At 1528 Carney gave another order: Form TG 34.5. Out of the Battle Line surged the superbattleships *Iowa* and *New Jersey* and such cruisers and destroyers as could keep up with them. We slowed briefly to give a couple of the destroyers a drink of our oil. Then we plunged ahead—fast, faster, fastest. All through his afternoon duty at the standup intelligence desk, John Marshall watched the speedometer in Flag Plot register a steady 30 knots. Then we stepped up to 35 knots, flank speed.

Of course we were too late. At 2100 the enemy force went through the strait—with but eighteen of the original thirty-two warships, and the mission to penetrate Leyte Gulf unaccomplished. Lagging behind was one destroyer left back to pick up survivors from the three heavy cruisers sunk by the jeep carrier pilots. TG 34.5 whooshed down to the strait just after midnight. Radars scanned, and *Iowa* signaled a skunk hugging the shore. Not a fit target for fast battleships, so cruisers went forward to take care of it. From the flag bridge we saw the arcing shells, then the bright explosion. Scratch one Japanese warship. On *New Jersey,* unrelieved dejection — not one gun fired. Not one gun fired in the whole Battle Line. End of "Bull's Run."

14

ROUT OF THE JAPANESE CARRIERS

CARRIERS! THIN-SKINNED AND LIGHTLY-GUNNED THOUGH they were, these swift monsters packed such power and range in their fighting planes that they had become the capital ships of the Pacific war. Halsey had been at sea on his flagship *Enterprise* when the Japanese carrier force struck Pearl Harbor and established the hegemony of the aircraft carrier. Halsey had then showed what the carrier task force could do when he led the first daring raids on the Japanese-held islands west of Hawaii, and when mightier flattops kept issuing from U.S. shipyards, it was Halsey's old South Pacific commander Mitscher who led the slashing raids that brought the United States back to the gates of the Philippines.

Now Halsey was back at sea, and Mitscher his carrier commander. Neither doubted that the Japanese, having committed their carriers, were now closing for the crucial blow of the fight for the Philippines — the swift annihilation of the main striking power of the enemy fleet, the carriers.

Mitscher's pilots had won the last carrier action in June when the enemy had sallied forth to meet the challenge of our invasion of the Marianas. Over our carriers and over Guam, Tinian, and Saipan, our airmen had downed hundreds of Japanese carrier planes. But in that battle few had seen — let alone attacked — the enemy carriers. That was because the enemy carriers had remained at a distance and, using the islands as bases, tried to shuttle-bomb our forces between, and when Mitscher's airmen broke up their game, they beat a retreat.

Of course we in Third Fleet didn't know that two Japanese carriers, torpedoed as they withdrew, had been sunk by our submarines in that battle. And though we had a pretty good idea that the Japanese might be running short of replacement pilots after the Marianas Turkey Shoot, we couldn't even know for sure that still other carriers might be lurking behind the four the enemy now risked to save the Philippines. But fresh in the mind of Mitscher's staff was yesterday's experience when TG 38.3, including their flagship *Lexington,* had come under attack by planes coming from the north. That attack had been broken up. But as searchers to the north then verified, the planes had come from the carriers—and those not shot down had flown on to land on Luzon. This suggested that the Japanese were back at their shuttle-bombing game and that, rearmed, refueled, and doubtless reinforced, the carrier planes could be expected back in the morning.

So both Halsey and Mitscher were bent on closing at high speed in the night and striking first to knock out the carriers before the Japanese could play their shuttle game again. And knocking them out early, before sending in our battleships to make 100 percent sure that no enemy carriers would get away this time. Mitscher put out the order to all three carrier groups to be ready to launch strikes immediately after sending out dawn searches. On all twelve carriers armorers worked through the night loading bombs and torpedoes. Pilots suited up early and sat waiting in their ready rooms. Every plane was pressed into service.

There was just enough light to catapult the first searchers at 0555. On a hunch that the enemy might have moved eastward, Mitscher called on *Essex,* launching its dawn CAP next, to vector four of these Hellcats out that way. This paid off richly. These speedy fighters were first to sight the enemy formation at 0710. Ducking away from interceptors that rose to meet them,

The fast carrier *Lexington*, with its ninety-six attack planes, served as
the flagship of Adm. Marc Mitscher's hard-charging Task Force 38.
After leading Halsey's carriers in smashing attacks on Okinawa,
Formosa, and the Philippines, Mitscher delivered the nearest thing to
a knockout in the three-day Leyte battle when on October 25 his
fliers destroyed the last remnants of Japan's carrier forces.

Lt. J. J. Collins not only flashed the first word but stayed on
over the target for more than an hour, and supplied an almost
completely accurate rundown of the enemy force's composition:
one *Zuikaku*-class carrier, two *Chitose*-class light carriers, one
Zuiho-class light carrier, two *Ise*-class battleships with flight
decks aft, one heavy cruiser, three light cruisers, and six destroyers. At our intelligence desk in Flag Plot we recognized at once
what Japanese naval messages our eavesdroppers sometimes succeeded in decoding called "Mobile Defense Force Main Body."

Smaller now than even one of Task Force 38's carrier groups, this shrunken remnant of the once conquering Strike Force that spread destruction from Hawaii to Ceylon was going to catch it.

Already, per Mitscher's order, all twelve carriers had launched deckload strikes, and several hundred planes were orbiting north of the force, awaiting only target information to deliver the day's first attack.

After Collins's early word, the strike coordinator, Cdr. David McCampbell from *Essex,* had only to lead them another hundred miles to the onslaught. They found the enemy ships already steaming in circular AA defense, the principal ships ranged in three columns with a thin screen of destroyers surrounding them. When McCampbell was still 10 miles away the defenders let fly their first flak. And high over the formation of warships flew some fifteen or twenty Zeke fighters. But these planes did not tangle with the attackers. Outnumbered, they went instead through stuntlike maneuvers, slow rolls, split Ss, and the like.

Not to be drawn off, the Hellcat escorts stuck with their dive bombers, but overshot when they followed the Helldivers down. Antiaircraft fire was intense, especially from the two battlewagons, but the bombers, zooming down one after the other, were not to be denied. They scored so many direct hits on a *Chitose*-class light carrier, including three below the waterline, that the ship reeled. A huge explosion obliterated the fantail. The whole ship caught fire and began to sink. It was gone by 0935.

Others in the first attack group claimed a possible hit on a *Zuiho*-class light carrier, which successfully evaded by a desperate turn. (Photo verification, markedly improved during the fight for Leyte, provided a gorgeous picture of this very moment.) The torpedo planes attacked last, dropping their fish from distances of 1,400 to 1,600 yards as the target ships went into tight turns. Many hits were claimed. One exploded against a destroyer, which sank almost at once, at 0835. One torpedo, launched by either an *Intrepid* or *San Jacinto* plane, was seen to hit *Zuikaku* squarely, and the big carrier took a list at once, apparently having trouble steering.

After following the dive bombers through their pullouts, the Hellcats turned to take on the Zekes, and the day's only dogfight took place. The enemy planes started with the altitude advantage. But the sturdy Hellcats could absorb more punishment than the Zekes, which caught fire readily when hit. On the first pass Lt. Joe Strane from *Essex* was able to get in full deflection bursts as a Zeke flashed by, and saw the plane crash in the water along with two other Zekes shot down by others. As he pulled out, Strane saw two Zekes firing on his wingman. Continuing his dive he pulled into position behind and above them and flamed both with only short 20-mm bursts. As he turned to shoot at a fourth, which started to smoke, another Zeke came at him head on, and its guns registered hits that started a fire between engine and cockpit. Strane's power failed. Another Zeke made a run on him, holing his port side and blowing away his instrument panel. Caught by the cockpit enclosure for a harrowing moment as the fire spread, he managed to wrest free at 2,000 feet and jumped. Entangled in the chute, he "swallowed a good deal of salt water," reported squadron ACI Joe McGinnis, "but lost it all with no trouble when in the raft."

From this vantage point Pilot Strane watched six successive deckload strikes fly over to maul the enemy ships, 350 planes by his count. In late afternoon a friendly destroyer hove into view. He flashed the little mirror in his survival kit, and the ship turned toward him. Picked up, dried out, he was found to have suffered only slight leg burns.

Strane's and one other were the only combat air losses for the whole day. And almost the first thing Lieutenant Collins reported as he circled high overhead was that the carriers below him were bare of planes. Of the fifteen or twenty that rose to meet the first attack, Strane and his comrades had splashed them all.

After that it was almost a processional as successive air coordinators coached in their attacks. As *Belleau Wood*'s Lt. Cdr. Vince Casey first saw the targets, the big carrier *Zuikaku* had just two planes spotted on the deck. And the two battleships with flight decks aft—this was our first glimpse of them—now proved to carry no planes whatsoever. But these freakish monsters could put up brisk AA fire, large-caliber phosphorus bursts in long white trailers as the bombers approached. When the torpedo planes went into their fast glides at 5,000 feet, the target ships would change course slightly, then go into drastic maneuvers as dive bombers and fighters roared down. When finally the torpedo planes bored in close, the defenders made their sharpest turns. Cruisers and battleships swung a full 180 degrees. Some were seen to be firing their main batteries at the low-flying Avengers.

This was the only strike in which TG 38.2's planes took part. Halsey, beginning to get distress calls from the south, was impatient to hear results. As early as 0850 he received Mitscher's TBS flash: one carrier sinking, two hit badly, only one still undamaged. Halsey had ordered Mitscher to "instruct pilots to attack undamaged ships," leaving cripples for his battleships to finish off. But by 1051 he was telling Admiral Bogan to hold his next strike on deck, and shortly afterward orders went out to TG 38.2 to turn south with Task Force 34 and furnish cover for the big ships as they rushed to help Kinkaid.

Halsey wasn't the only one to reverse course that morning. This time it was the Japanese—trying to pull off their shuttle-bombing stunt again. They failed utterly. At 0957 TG 38.4 radars detected a sizable bogey approaching from Luzon. *San Jacinto* fighters were vectored out to intercept them. If indeed these were the planes that, failing to break through TG 38.3's fighter defense yesterday, had flown on to Luzon, they showed no more stomach for a fight this time. TG 38.4's fighters gave chase, and the would-be attackers turned and ran for Luzon.

All through the rest of the day, the two remaining groups of

Task Force 38 sent attacks at the Japanese carrier force. To the leader of Strike Two, "the enemy force presented a picture of wild confusion." This time both *Lexington* and *Franklin* bombers scored hits on the evasive light carrier identified later in the day as *Zuiho*. *San Jacinto* and *Belleau Wood* attackers damaged a light cruiser, which had to drop out of the formation. Lt. C. O. Roberts, the next strike coordinator watching from overhead, radioed that it took the target ships 45 minutes to straighten out after his group's strike. Destroyers were bunched around the least damaged carriers, a battleship was trying to take a stricken light carrier in tow, and the wounded cruiser was trailing oil.

Then came Strike 3, the day's heaviest. Its coordinator was Cdr. Hugh Winters from *Lexington*. By this time cloud cover had spread over the target ships, effectively lessening the flak the defenders could throw up. Lacking fire control radars on their guns and aiming visually, the Japanese gun crews had to hold their fire until the attacking planes were already upon them. In this attack, which struck between 1330 and 1400, not a single pilot or plane suffered injury. Planes from *Lexington, Essex,* and *Langley* zeroed in on *Zuikaku* and the light carrier *Zuiho*. Although *Zuikaku* had recovered sufficiently to keep station, the big ship now caught it. No fewer than seven torpedoes found their mark, and the dive bombers, sweeping down through ineffectual machine-gun fire, planted seven direct hits that blew holes in the flight deck. Huge fires spread, and at 1412 *Zuikaku,* last surviving member of the carrier force that attacked Pearl Harbor, rolled over and sank. Nor did *Zuiho* escape this time. Two torpedoes exploded on the ship's port side, one bomb holed the flight deck, and a dozen near misses caused still more damage both belowdeck and topside, and *Zuiho* was seen to go under at 1526. The light carrier described as undamaged in Mitscher's morning flash report also took hits that compelled the vessel to drop back, dead in the water.

Almost as many near-misses grazed the two battleships, but these heavy ships seemed to shake them off as they led the re-

treat northward. Strike 4 bombs straddled them close enough to
blow airplane cranes off the fantail. *Franklin* kept sending in
attacks—our carriers were now no more than 40 miles from the
nearest stragglers—until "Big Ben" had only a single torpedo
left. *Belleau Wood* ran out of torpedoes. At 1610 TG 38.3's last
strike counted ten ships still afloat, including the now derelict
fourth carrier. They confirmed the earlier sinking of the destroyer and claimed a 250-pound bomb hit on the stern of a
cruiser. Once again the battleships dodged torpedoes and, en-
gulfed in smoke and spray from bombs exploding close aboard,
slowed momentarily, then resumed speed. *Enterprise* won permission to launch sixteen fighters with 1,000-pound bombs for
one last shot at a cruiser. They missed in the dim light and had
to make night landings on their return.

Their purpose was to add targets for Mitscher's mop-up crew.
These were light surface forces that Task Force 38's commander
ordered to prepare to go forward and do the job that Halsey had
intended for the heavies of Task Force 34. At 1753 we heard in
Flag Plot as we sped south that Mitscher was detaching Cruiser
Division 13 for the job.

By that hour what was left of the enemy's Main Body—the
two battlewagons, a couple of cruisers, and some screening destroyers—had pulled well ahead. But the fourth carrier was still
afloat with a few destroyers standing by. Commander Winters,
in his Hellcat, was still trying to keep track of the fleeing enemy,
sketching their positions on his kneepad after seven hours in the
air. Pausing in his return to *Lexington,* he guided the cruisers to
the derelict Japanese carrier, and even spotted their splashes for
them as they took the ship under fire. From the deck of the ship
that had rescued him, Lieutenant Strane watched the conclud-
ing action of a day his three kills and one probable had begun.
Shooting six-inch shells point-blank at the carrier, identified
from the day's photographs as *Chiyoda,* they made short work of
it. Within a half hour this last of the enemy carrier force turned
over and sank beneath the waves.

Bending on speed the cruisers gave chase to the vessels that had been trying to help the carrier. One spunky destroyer stayed to fight it out.

When light cruiser *Mobile* opened fire at 1853, the outgunned enemy not only returned fire but swung around as if to launch a spread of torpedoes. This forced the cruisers to turn away and gave the other Japanese ships a chance to escape. Admiral Du-Bose, commanding, then laid on speed up to 28 knots. At 1915 his ships caught up with the scrappy destroyer. At a distance of only 6,000 yards the cruisers then pumped deliberate, methodical fire until the destroyer exploded and sank at 2059.

And so Admiral Mitscher and his men finished by the light of the cruisers' star shells what they had begun at dawn. All told, our fast carriers flew 637 sorties to wipe out the Japanese carrier force. Thus Task Force 38's primary mission had been accomplished, even though Admiral Halsey's goal of annihilating the entire Mobile Fleet lost out. That, as was already beginning to become clear, was because the battle for Leyte was so much bigger than this last carrier engagement of the Pacific war. Already while the exulting dispatches flooded in from the carrier forces, the strange absence of opposing aircraft was raising doubts in Flag Plot about why these capital ships had been so recklessly exposed—and expended.

Ten of the enemy force's seventeen ships, led by the two hardshell battlewagons, made it back to Japan. But not the light cruiser *Tama*. Sufficiently recovered from a direct hit by Mitscher's fliers to have limped beyond the range of our cruiser mop-up party, this ship plodding its solitary way northwards fell into the jaws of a waiting U.S. wolfpack. Together the submarines *Jallao* and *Pintado* stalked the lone survivor. Taking aim at the three-stack cruiser in the misty moonlight, *Jallao* fired seven torpedoes, three of which hit, and *Pintado*'s skipper watched the ship go down just before midnight of the third day of history's biggest seafight.

15

PURSUIT

"THE PURSUIT PHASE OF THE BATTLE IS NOW IN PROGRESS," proclaimed Admiral Halsey.

In the north there were no carriers left to pursue, and it was the submarines that tracked down the cripples: *Jallao* finished off the limping cruiser *Tama* with three torpedo hits. To the south long-legged Air Force bombers from Morotai and New Guinea located the crippled light cruiser *Abukuma* and sank that fugitive from the Surigao slaughter with a neat, tight bomb pattern on a target that was unable to dodge anymore.

In the central Philippines, Halsey could not muster the full force of Task Force 38's hitting power because two fast carrier groups, having attacked the Japanese carrier force until dark on October 25, were too far north to join the chase for the retreating Striking Force. But he had sent Admiral McCain's TG 38.1 flying to aid the beleaguered escort carriers off Samar, and Admiral Bogan's TG 38.2 had turned south to cover Halsey's battleship rush for San Bernardino. Accordingly, these were the carrier groups, already stretched near the limit, that Halsey now called upon to search westward at dawn October 26 and carry out "sustained strikes" to destroy the fleeing Striking Force. Admiral McCain, he said, would be in charge.

McCain's airmen had had to fly the longest strikes of the war the day before, and a good many had had to come down at Tacloban or ditch in the sea trying to make it back to their

ships. But McCain's five carriers and Bogan's three still added up
to a considerable force, and they sent off their first searches and
sweeps, including Avengers armed with torpedoes, at dawn. Pilots, said McCain, should "listen for contacts from the searchers and kick hell out of those ships."

At 0810 their leader found the enemy formation in Tablas
Strait and McCain immediately sent off a second strike. And by
0850 they were attacking the Striking Force whose ships, still
including four fast battleships, put up a stiff AA barrage and
went into radical evasive maneuvers. McCain's airmen claimed
two torpedo and "many" bomb hits on a *Nagato*-type battleship, and bomb hits on the huge *Yamato*.

One target, later identified as *Kumano*, the heavy cruiser
whose bow had been blown off in the Samar engagement the
day before, had somehow managed to keep up with the rest up
to this point. Now the attacking airmen subjected this ship to a
veritable blitz, claiming torpedo and bomb hits, one of which
exploded after penetrating the main deck. That left the cruiser
helpless, unable to keep up with the Main Body any longer.
They also hit and slowed a light cruiser, which dropped behind
with a destroyer escorting.

At 1030 planes of Air Group Seven from *Hancock* closed for
a coordinated attack. They sighted seven Zekes, about the only
enemy planes seen all day, but these hung back and made no
attempt to intercept. Fighter-bombers pushed over from 10,000
feet. The first was hit at once by flak and crashed. The rest
hurtled down at the target ships, strafing the defenders' guns as
they dived. And just as they released their 500-pound bombs,
six torpedo planes glided in out of the sun. As the action report
recounted, the attackers

> swung around to the north and west of the target to make
> an anvil attack from both bows. Lt. (jg) Hunt and Ensign
> Reynolds approached on the starboard side, released their
> torpedoes almost simultaneously at an angle of about
> 075 on the target, and their torpedoes ran parallel about

200 feet apart. The cruiser could not maneuver out of the
way at her slow speed. Hunt's torpedo hit at a point on a line
with the second forward turret and Reynolds' passed a few
feet forward of the bow. Lieut. Brewer and Ensign Morey
had difficulty getting clear of the destroyer on the port bow.
Their torpedoes were launched almost head-on to the target and one passed on the port side and the other was a
sinker.

Hunt's hit caused a terrific explosion with two succeeding
explosions and a burst of flame from the opened starboard
side. The ship almost immediately began to list heavily and
settle on the starboard bow. As the last planes left, the forward turrets were awash and a high pillar of flames and smoke
poured from the forward part of the ship.

This was the light cruiser *Noshiro,* seen to sink shortly afterward
at 1137. The heavy cruiser, claimed probably sunk, survived. Left
behind with an escorting destroyer, the ship staggered westward
and took refuge in Coron Bay.

This was also the day that the U.S. Army Air Forces, which
had earlier scored a knockout in the Sulu Sea, got into the act
against the Striking Force. A few minutes after the second strike
by McCain's airmen, a formation of forty-seven Morotai-based
B-24s put in an appearance over the remaining heavy ships. Flying at high altitude, wheeling deliberately and ponderously to
pick their targets, they delivered two attacks. They claimed
eight hits on two battleships and a cruiser. Their bomb salvo of
150 thousand-pounders caused plenty of damage even with
near-misses.

Eventually, the Japanese remnants crept beyond carrier-plane
range, and Admiral Bogan reported his planes' afternoon (third)
strike negative. But before the day was over Task Force 38 bombers caught two destroyers alone in the Mindoro area, sinking
one and forcing the other to beach on Semirara Island, south of
Mindoro.

In Flag Plot we totted up the score. During the last day Task

Force 38 had sent 257 planes to the attack, only three less than employed against the same enemy force as it advanced through the same waters two days before. The day's attacks had knocked out four more ships of the Striking Force. Thus, of the thirty-two warships that had set forth from Brunei Bay on October 22—and failed in their mission to destroy the U.S. invasion—a force of four battered battleships, four limping cruisers, and a scattering of destroyers, perhaps fifteen ships in all—ended up back at Brunei on October 28. (The two detailed action reports prepared by ACIs in Flag Plot and dispatched to Nimitz and MacArthur, with information copy to Commander-in-Chief King, are printed in the appendix, along with Third Fleet's War Diary evaluation of losses inflicted on the enemy in the battle for Leyte.)

For their part, at the end of "Bull's Run" on the evening of October 25, Halsey and Carney fired off a don't-tread-on-me dispatch to Nimitz and MacArthur, information copy to Kinkaid and King in Washington. In tone as well as substance it set forth much more than a defense of Third Fleet's actions. "That there be no misunderstanding concerning operations," it began, "I inform you as follows"—and proceeded to state how Third Fleet engaged both attacking surface forces on October 24 and could see that a coordinated enemy movement was under way —but "the expected enemy carrier force was missing from the picture." Late afternoon searches found the enemy carrier force "completing the picture."

At this point, "to statically guard San Bernardino Strait while subject to enemy surface and carrier attacks, would have been childish." So, said Halsey, he concentrated his carrier forces in the night and started north for a surprise dawn attack on the enemy fleet.

> I considered that the enemy force in Sibuyan Sea had been so badly damaged that they constituted no serious threat to Kinkaid—and that estimate has been borne out by the events of the 25th off Surigao.

Com 7th Fleet's urgent appeals for help came at a time when the enemy was heavily damaged and my overwhelming surface striking force was within 45 miles of the enemy cripples. I had no alternative but to break off from my golden opportunity and head south though I was convinced that his force was adequate to deal with an enemy that was badly weakened by our attacks of the 24th a conviction justified by later events off Leyte.

I wish to point out that MacArthur and Kinkaid were supported by A) Destruction of 1200 enemy planes between 10 and 20 October plus much shipping. B) Air attacks against Jap forces in the Sulu Sea. C) Crippling of enemy force in Sibuyan Sea. D) Destruction of over 150 planes on 24 October. E) Destruction of enemy carrier strength on 25 October. F) Carrier attacks on threatening enemy force off Leyte 25 October. G) Surface movements evening 25 October to cut off enemy retreat toward San Bernardino.

And a final shot:

The back of the Jap Navy has been broken in the course of supporting our landings at Leyte.

Third Fleet, too, had been through an ordeal. It had lost only one ship in the battle, the light carrier *Princeton.* But its airmen had been driven to the limit. After the heavy actions off Formosa, Fighter Squadron Eight was reported to be suffering practically 100 percent from combat fatigue. On the eve of the Battle of Leyte Gulf, Halsey sent the big carrier *Bunker Hill* back to the rear with orders to relieve the entire Air Group Eight. Halsey had to caution McCain to refrain from including statistics about decline in combat readiness among his pilots in his dispatches. And Mitscher, relinquishing Task Force 38 command to McCain after the battle, wrote in his action report:

Currently our carrier air groups are being debilitated by extended periods of combat duty under ship-based conditions.

Ships of Task Force 38 have been under constant pressure. Probably 10,000 men have never set foot on shore during this period. No other force in the world has been subjected to such a period of constant operation without rest. The reactions of the crews are slowed down.

Two of our four fast carrier groups, TG 38.1 and TG 38.3, now retired to Ulithi, and Kinkaid's baby flattops, those that survived, staggered back to Manus Island for repairs. Halsey would not be taking off on any thousand-plane strike on Tokyo in November. MacArthur and Nimitz agreed that the fast carriers, at least two groups, must stay and fly cover at Leyte at least until MacArthur's air force got ashore and organized for the job.

What really had been at stake at Leyte? Surely it could not have been said of Halsey at Leyte, as Churchill said of Jellicoe at Jutland, that he was the only man who could have lost the war in an afternoon. By the fall of 1944 there simply was no stopping the mighty war machine that America had mobilized to fight across both Atlantic and Pacific. Any country that could simultaneously mount great invasions in Europe and East Asia was far too preponderant to be in danger of losing. Indeed, any country that could deploy sixteen smaller carriers mounting 550 attack planes as an unprogrammed reserve had little to fear from the warships that tried to break through to the Leyte invasion beach. Even when those ships were unaccountably allowed to get close enough to fire on them—and the enemy launched shore-based suicide attacks in support—our "backup" carrier force not only stood off their attack but routed them. No thanks to Admiral Halsey, though. This was a Seventh Fleet success. As at least three of Halsey's top commanders said later (two of them at the time), he should have left Task Force 34 and a covering carrier group to block San Bernardino Strait while dispatching the main strength of Task Force 38 north to engage and destroy the Japanese carriers. But Halsey, by leaving San Bernardino Strait open, turned Leyte into what Wellington called Waterloo—"a damned close-run thing."

Afterward, stern old Ernie King, possibly mindful that as one of the Joints Chiefs he was responsible for the split command at Leyte, never criticized Halsey. He did express dissatisfaction that Kinkaid neglected to send searches northward, and that left the jeep carriers open to the unthinkable, namely attack by surface ships. Also Admiral Nimitz, possibly because of his uncharacteristic intervention in midbattle, asking "Where is Task Force 34?"—thereby forcing Halsey to lead those ships in their futile, wild-goose chase after the withdrawing enemy ships—kept his counsel afterward as to Halsey's actions. Admiral Kinkaid certainly felt let down by Halsey's leaving the strait unguarded. He smoldered for years thereafter. But later, when he was postwar commander of the Eastern Sea Frontier, Carney went up to New York and put it to him that as young men they had seen the damage done to the Navy's good name by the unseemly squabbling between admirals Sampson and Schley about their respective performances in the Spanish-American War. Whatever Kinkaid's thoughts, he never published his book as almost all the rest of them did.

Halsey, of course, went right on, leading his Third Fleet in marauding raids up and down the China Sea and then, shifting his flag to *New Jersey*'s sister ship *Missouri,* against Japan itself. He won his fifth star and the title of fleet admiral. On the eve of V-J day, after the Japanese sued for peace, he was still advising his pilots, if they encountered enemy planes, to "shoot them down in a friendly sort of way." He never had to make good on his South Pacific boast that he'd ride the emperor's white horse into Tokyo (although there was an abortive move in his staff to land and seize the beast for him). Instead he had the satisfaction of seeing the Japanese surrender aboard his flagship on September 2, 1945.

Halsey proposes a toast at the wedding of Lieutenant Cox and Molly
Claridge. "In a colorful ceremony Admiral Halsey, commander of
the famous Third Fleet, gave away the bride," reported the *Honolulu
Advertiser* on October 5, 1944.

AFTERWORD

THE FOREGOING MEMOIR, WHILE DRAWING ON THIRD FLEET action reports and interviews, tells only what we knew at the time. We did not even know the names of the Japanese admirals opposing us, or the identity of the ships they led against us. Nor did we know they were operating under the so-called SHO-Plan—which happened to adopt the very strategic outline first set forth in Admiral Koga's Z-Plan.

But between May and October of 1944 the Japanese suffered heavy losses of pilots trying to prevent our capture of the Marianas, and also loss of three aircraft carriers. As a result the flat-tops dispatched from Japan to oppose us in October carried a much smaller complement of pilots and planes, and the SHO-Plan assigned them an explicitly diversionary role.

Of course we did not know this. Nor had we seen a captured document circulated by our naval intelligence about that time that spoke of "decoy" tactics for elements of the Japanese carrier force.

It was altogether Harris Cox's analysis of the Z-Plan's priorities in our cabin on *New Jersey* that enabled two of us juniors to divine, that fateful night of October 24, that the Japanese were desperately exposing, and expending, their carriers to draw us away and enable the surface ships to get by and do their job.

After the war the Navy dropped Air Combat Intelligence. "Too narrow," the brass said. Well, all of us ACIs were reservists,

After switching his flag from *New Jersey* to sister ship *Missouri*,
Halsey decorated many members of the Third Fleet staff, including
the author.

sometime sailors, and the Navy no longer needed us. And
I couldn't contest that judgment after I saw the get-the-
carriers frenzy the night Third Fleet left San Bernardino Strait
unguarded.

Cox left us only months later in Honolulu and shortly mar-
ried Mollie Claridge, a great favorite of us all in Noumea and a
New Zealander who had found new volunteer service-canteen
work in Hawaii. At the wedding, Admiral Halsey gave the bride
away. After the war Harris and Mollie were spending an evening
with the admiral in Washington when Harris happened to say,
"Admiral, you made a big mistake. . . ." Halsey himself had said
as much at one time or another (he used to say he should have
commanded at the Battle of the Philippine Sea—and Spruance at Leyte). But he was so startled by Harris's remark that he
dropped his cigarette behind a pillow and nearly set the sofa on
fire.

Harris died in 1965. I last saw Halsey in 1959, by which time his eyes were dimmed by double-cataract surgery, his wide shoulders bent, his gait unsteady. But when we recalled his message from Noumea to the carriers in the dark days of 1942, "Attack Repeat Attack," his face lit up. He died two months later. I last saw Admiral Carney when a few of us met in 1985 to mark the fortieth anniversary of the Japanese surrender on Third Fleet's flagship in Tokyo Bay. Bent like a question mark at 88 and long retired as Chief of Naval Operations, he said he had put his version of the Battle of Leyte out of bounds until after his death. In 1992 I came upon his oral history at Columbia University. When his version comes to the night of October 24, 1944, he says, "Let others tell the story."

Now, fifty years afterward, I do so.

APPENDIX

From the Third Fleet Dispatch Board:

241104 HALSEY to CINCPAC, CINCSOWESPAC, info
COMINCH:

On 24th launched strong dawn search teams from three
groups across Luzon and the Visayas. At 0745 search planes
contacted enemy force 4 BB. 8 CA 2 CL 13 DD fifteen
miles south of Mindoro. 38.3 and 38.4 struck same force
after initial strikes on other targets. 38.3 reported 1 CA 1 CL
1 DD Manila Bay all damaged (estimate some damaged by
Blue subs). After first strike 38.3 under heavy air attack and
shot down about 150 planes. *Princeton* damaged and dead in
water. *Birmingham* had personnel casualties resulting from
explosion aboard *Princeton* while alongside her. 38.4 first
strike enemy force southeast of Negros consisting of 2 *Fuso*
class battleships, 1 CA, 4 DD making two bomb hits on
each BB, rocket hits on CA and 2 DD, strafed 2 remaining
DD. None of these seen to sink.

Main Body reversed course to 270 about 1400 when 30
miles west of Tablas island and while again being attacked.
Main Body score from incomplete reports: 1 *Yamato* class
bombed torpedoed left afire and down at bow. *Kongo* class 2
bomb hits left smoking and apparently badly damaged.
Bomb hits on one or both remaining BB, 2 torpedo hits on
one of these bombed BB. 1 CL torpedoed and capsized.
Torpedo hits on 2 CA and bomb hits on another CA.

At 1540 search planes from 38.3 sighted enemy force near 18 10N 125 30E report evaluated as 2 *Ise* class, 2 CA 1 CL 6 DD c. 210 speed 15. At 1640 another group sighted 18 25N 125 28E 2 *Zuikaku,* 1 CVL, 1 CL 3 DD course 270 speed 12. 2 DD 100 miles NE this group course 240. Planes from this force may have been attacking 38.3 prior to contact.

CTG 38.3 has scuttled *Princeton* and is now closing 38.2 and 38.4 which are now concentrating off entrance to San Bernardino Strait. More later.

251439   Continuing my 241104. Ten planes shot down on 24th by TG 38.2 CAP and search planes. 25th activities: Three groups concentrated for early morning attack on enemy carrier force near 18 25N 125 30E. Negligible air opposition at target and no strikes on own force.

First strike one carrier, type uncertain, exploded and sunk. One CV and 1 CVL hit with one torpedo and three bombs each, and one CL badly damaged. Upon recovery of second strike, TF 34 and TG 38.2 departed for Leyte in response to TF 77 report of critical situation. TG 38.3 and 38.4 continued afternoon air strikes and probable night surface action against carrier forces. TG 38.1 made morning strike on enemy forces east of Samar, leaving 1 BB, 1 CA and 1 DD dead in water. The CA apparently in sinking condition. Three other heavy ships damaged.

At 2140 search planes reported 14 ships San Bernardino entrance course 270. The remainder of 27 ships sighted east of Mindoro morning of 24th but conflicting reports prevent estimate of number which sortied from San Bernardino.

From Third Fleet's War Diary:

The evaluation of [enemy] losses: In the three days Oct 24, 25 and 26, follows:

Northern Force

3 CV sunk by carrier planes
1 CVL damaged by carrier planes, sunk by cruisers

1 XCV-BB *Ise* damaged by 2 torpedo hits and number of bomb hits
1 XCV-BB *Hyuga* damaged by a number of bomb hits
1 CA *Ashigara* class damaged by bomb hits
1 CL *Natori* class damaged by bombs, later sunk by subs
1 CL *Oyodo* slightly damaged by bombs
1 CL *Tama* damaged by bombs, probably sunk
1 CL not damaged
6 DD 1 sunk by carrier planes; 1 damaged by carrier planes, sunk by
   cruisers, 1 damaged by bombs; 2 damaged by heavy strafing
1 DD undamaged

Center Force

1 BB *Musashi* hit with 2 or more torpedoes and numerous bombs.
   Last seen afire and down by bow, dead in water in Sibuyan sea.
   Not seen again and believed sunk.
1 BB *Yamato* damaged by 1 or more torpedoes and numerous bombs
   incl. 2 half-ton SAP and rockets on 24 Oct.
1 BB *Nagato* damaged by 1 torpedo Oct 24, 1 torpedo Oct 26.
1 BB *Kongo* damaged by 2 torpedoes Oct 24, 1 torpedo on Oct 26,
   numerous bombs.
1 BB *Haruna* damaged by numerous bomb hits on Oct 24, 25, 26.
   Not more than one of latter seen after Oct 26, and it is possible
   that either (*Kongo, Haruna*) sank on or after Oct 26.
1 CA *Kumano* torpedoed on Oct 24 and seriously damaged. Did not
   sortie with the force.
1 CA *Haguro* torpedoed. Did not sortie. Possibly sunk.
1 CA *Suzuya* damaged by bomb hit on 24th, sunk east of Samar.
1 CA *Chikuma* damaged with 1 torpedo on 24th, sunk on 25th in
   combined attack.
1 CA *Tone* damaged by 1 torpedo, apparently not serious.
1 CA *Chokai* damaged by bomb hit on 24th, additional bomb hits on
   25th, damaged by torpedo hit on 26th.
1 CL torpedoed, rolled over and sank Oct 24th.
1 CL damaged by bomb hits Oct 24th, 25th.
13 DD 2 DD sunk, 1 by cruiser fire at San Bernardino, 1 by carrier
   planes Oct 25th, 7 DD damaged, mostly minor strafing or near-
   misses. 5 DD not damaged.

Southern Force

1 BB *Fuso* hit by bombs, rockets and set afire Oct 24th—later sunk by 7th Fleet in Surigao.

1 BB *Yamashiro* bomb hits, minor damage—later sunk by Seventh Fleet in Surigao.

1 CL *Agano* type damaged by strafing.

4 DD damaged by strafing.

Miscellaneous Forces

MANILA HARBOR

1 CL damaged Oct 24th by bomb hits and strafing by TG 38.3 planes.

1 DD damaged by bomb hits and strafing.

TABLAS AREA

DD: 1 sunk, 1 probably sunk, 1 damaged by rockets and strafing by TG 38.4 planes 24th Oct.

NOTES

I. CROSSING THE POPE'S LINE

6   "29 planes bombed Munda": John F. Marshall, "Wartime Experiences," mimeo (1974), 56; revised as *Civilian in Uniform,* privately printed, 1994.

9   "COMCONFORSOLS": J. Bryan III in *Saturday Evening Post,* December 25, 1943.

11   Palau invasion photos: Marshall, "Wartime Experiences," 57.

15   Nimitz directive to Halsey: CINCPOA Operation Plan 8-44, dated September 27, 1944 (hereafter CINCPOA OP PLAN 8-44).

20   *Washington* shells "right on": Ivan Musicant, *Battleship at War: Epic Story of USS Washington* (New York: Harcourt Brace Jovanovich, 1986), 134.

20   "like sitting on a pogo stick": Ibid., 137.

21   *New Jersey's* extra-long bow: Marshall, "Wartime Experiences," 63.

21   that grace and majesty could coexist: Robert F. Dorr, *The New Jersey: The Navy's Big Guns* (Osceola, Wis.: Motorbooks International Publishers, 1988), 22.

21   "Bulletin for Officers": Solberg, "World War Journal," unpaged scrapbook, author's personal collection.

23   "Pity those things were invented": Ibid.

25   "What type of ship are you?" Ibid.

26   like being hit by a slow truck: Malcolm Muir, *The Iowa-class Battleships* (Poole, Dorsetshire, England: Blandford Press, 1987), 39.

26   "Thank goodness you're here": Ibid., 43.

28   "Lieut. Solberg, ACI officer": Third Fleet War Diary, September 15, 1944.
28   caught "with their flaps down": *Admiral Halsey's Story* (New York: McGraw-Hill, 1947).

2. THE LIMITS OF OUR KNOWLEDGE

35   "Large flight of planes . . . we hoped": Marshall, "Wartime Experiences," 24.
36   "Good hunting": Quoted in David Kahn, *The Codebreakers* (New York: Macmillan, 1967), 599.
37   "Pop goes the weasel": quoted in John Toland, *The Rising Sun* (New York: Bantam Books, 1971), 502.
37   "Hold on, Kelly": *Admiral Halsey's Story,* 208.

3. PROTEAN PRELIMINARIES

41   "I can't see": Cato Tillar, interview with author.
42   "good old Sara": Solberg, "World War Journal." See also Stanley Johnston, *The Grim Reapers* (New York: E. P. Dutton, 1943), 40, 45, 212.
50   "Raid Two . . .": J. Bryan III, *Aircraft Carrier* (New York: Ballantine Books, 1954), 94.
51   "an alltime naval record": Quoted in Thomas L. Morrissey, "Odyssey of Fighting Two," mimeo (1945), 15.
52   "We came down from 17,000 feet": Ensign Tillar's logbook.
54   "Downed carrier pilot rescued": Third Fleet action report, Enclosure A, dated November 13, 1944.
54   "Having the utmost confidence": *General Marshall's Report: Winning the War in Europe and the Pacific* (New York: Simon and Schuster, 1945).
55   "We achieved total surprise": Halsey oral history, March 29, 1944.
56   "They knew we were coming": Task Force 38 action report, dated November 3, 1944.
56   "I should have struck Formosa first": *Admiral Halsey's Story,* 205.
57   "a knock-down drag-out fight": S. E. Morison, *History of U.S. Naval Operations in World War II* (Boston: Little, Brown, 1958), 12:95.
59   "inflict lasting damage on . . . Formosa": Third Fleet action report.
59   "found it impossible to destroy": Task Force 38 action report.
60   "He still did not turn": Quoted in John W. Alexander, "Flight Quarters: The War Story of the Belleau Wood," mimeo (1946), 47.

64   "dirty tricks department": *Admiral Halsey's Story,* 235. Also "War Comes
     Back to the Philippines," *Life,* October 30, 1944.

64   "that if opportunity offer": CINCPOA OP PLAN 8-44.

65   "retiring toward the enemy": *Admiral Halsey's Story,* 208.

65   "the country has followed": Ibid., 209.

66   "a sad picture": Quoted in Commo. Richard Bates, *Strategic and Tac-
     tical Analysis, Leyte,* 3:114.

66   "Negative . . . responsible seniors instil": Third Fleet action report.
     Also Bates, *Strategic and Tactical Analysis, Leyte,* 3:114, 336.

66   "Damn it all, I know": Quoted in Marshall, "Wartime Experiences," 74.

4. THE SUBMARINES

68   "In case of opportunity": CINCPOA OP PLAN 8-44.

69   "Contact": McClintock, interview with author.

71   *Darter* contact report: Third Fleet action report.

73   "Officers never listen": Quoted by Lieutenant Brady, interview with
     author.

75   "the destruction of merchant shipping": CINCPAC action report, 1944.

76   "Consider primary mission": Bates, *Strategic and Tactical Analysis,* 1:177.

77   CINCPAC estimate regarding carriers: Third Fleet action report.

77   "many radars": *Darter* War Patrol report, dated November 5, 1944.

77   "He's trackin' 'em": Doug Moulton, interview with author. Other Sep-
     tember 23 comments: Wilson and Carney, interviews with author;
     Carney, "Narrative Report," mimeo (March 1945). Also Carney oral
     history; Ralph J. Wilson, "Remarks on Operations in the Western Pa-
     cific at the Naval War College," mimeo (Fall 1946).

79   Enemy naval challenge for Leyte not expected: Nimitz 0127 to Halsey
     October 12 in Third Fleet action report. MacArthur's Operations In-
     structions #70, dated September 21, 1944. SWPA Intelligence sum-
     mary, dated October 21, 1944.

80   "I regard the approach of enemy combatant ships": Third Fleet action
     report.

80   Third Fleet *must* support MacArthur: Ibid.

80   "swing some blows": Ibid.

81   "I had sense enough": Halsey Papers, Library of Congress.

81   "No operation plan can ever include": Carney, "Narrative Report."

83   "Important messages coming": Charles M. Fox Jr., letter to author.

5. THE SEAFIGHT BEGINS

85 "The tracking party plotted": McClintock, interview with author.

85 "The targets began to pop up": Claggett, interview with author.

86 "The second reason we ran": Ibid.

86 "*Darter* was to attack": McClintock, interview with author.

86 "Breaking out oars": *Darter* War Patrol report.

86 "It got up to 20 ships": Claggett, interview with author.

86 "kept looking at that big radar pip": McClintock, interview with author.

86 "I could see in their eyes": Ibid.

87 "Reversed course": *Darter* War Patrol report.

89 "Five more torpedo hits": *Dace* War Patrol report, dated November 6, 1944.

92 "Was this the one?": McClintock, interview with author.

93 "Heard slight explosion": *Dace* War patrol report.

94 "The only way I can get a seat": R. C. Benitez, "Battle Stations Submerged," *Naval Institute Proceedings* (January 1948).

94 "couldn't get Commander McClintock out": Claggett, interview with author.

94 "We were happy": Benitez, "Battle Stations Submerged."

6. THE KNOCKOUT THAT WASN'T

97 "Splash one Emily": Third Fleet action report.

97 "Much enemy activity suggests": Task Group 38.3 action report, dated December 2, 1944.

99 "I see 'em, big ships": Solberg, "World War Journal."

99 "Four battleships . . .": Third Fleet action report.

99 "Never in any main action": Carney, "Narrative Report."

100 "Commander First Striking Fleet unlocated but": Third Fleet action report.

100 "Carriers not located": Ibid.

101 "Many planes around": Task Force 38 action report.

102 "In the next hour or so": Air Group 15 action report, dated November 11, 1944.

103 "a spectacle terrible to behold": Quoted in Morison, *History of U.S. Naval Operations in World War II*, 12:181.

104 "Strike rpt strike!": Third Fleet action report.

105   "I saw that damned pagoda": *Intrepid* action report.

108   "The enemy's course to the west": TG 38.2 action report, dated November 8, 1944.

108   "Enemy force on easterly . . . westerly": TG 38.4 action report, dated November 19, 1944.

108   "Main Body reversed course": Third Fleet action report.

7. THE JAPANESE CARRIERS ARRIVE

111   "Enemy carrier strength not located": Third Fleet action report.

111   "The enemy pilots were the most aggressive": Air Group 15 action report.

112   "strongly suspicious": TG 38.3 action report.

112   "got a good look": Third Fleet action report.

113   "New contact": Ibid.

8. DECISION

114   Major forces of the Japanese fleet: Third Fleet action report.

115   "could see that a major coordinated enemy movement": Ibid.

115   "Task Force 34 engages decisively": Ibid.

115   "Operate in this vicinity": Ibid.

115   "completed the picture": Ibid.

116   "two *Zuikaku*-class": Task Force 38 action report.

116   "Main Body score": Third Fleet action report.

116   "Planes from this force may": Ibid.

118   "I might have had other ideas": Carney oral history.

118   "Here's where we're going, Mick": *Admiral Halsey's Story*, 217.

118   "Proceed at best speed": Third Fleet action report.

119   "Enemy force Sibuyan Sea": Ibid.

9. DISSENT

121   Z Operation Orders: ATIS Limited Distribution Translation No. 4, dated May 23, 1944.

124   "Bear in mind": Ibid., 18.

125   "They're coming through, I know": McMillan, interview with author.

125   "until it reached the southern tip": *Independence* action report, dated November 2, 1944.

126   "Yes, yes, we have that information": Adm. Gerald Bogan, oral history.

10. SLAUGHTER AT SURIGAO

129   "Never give a sucker an even break": Quoted in Morison, *History of U.S. Naval Operations in World War II*, 12:202.
131   "The arched line of tracers": Desron 10 action report.
132   "an entirely different enemy force": Identified in radio intercepts as "Second Attack Force." Third Fleet action report.
133   "burning like a city block": Quoted in Morison, *History of U.S. Naval Operations in World War II*, 12:236.

11. JEEP CARRIERS SAVE THE DAY

137   "shooting at us in Technicolor": Quoted in Morison, *History of U.S. Naval Operations in World War II*, 12:253.
137   "the volume and accuracy of the fire": TU 77.4.3 action report.
137   "in the ultimate circumstances": Ibid.
138   "the heroic efforts of her crew": Ibid.
139   "We circled the heavy cruisers": *Kitkun Bay* action report.
139   "Goddamit, boys, they're getting away": Clifton Sprague in *American Magazine*, April 1945.
139   "I could not believe my eyes": Ibid.

12. THE KAMIKAZES

143   "We were bubbling": Quoted in Hatsho Naito, *Thunder Gods* (Tokyo: Kadansha International, 1989), 25.
144   "I will end my story": Home Box Office TV documentary, "Kamikaze: Mission of Death," 1990.
144   "Grow up and be a healthy and big girl": Ibid.
147   "one of the most vicious enemy attacks": *Enterprise* action report, dated November 3, 1944.
148   "We were fighting for our lives": Ibid.

13. BULL'S RUN

149   "Due to our commitment to the south": Third Fleet action report.
149   "have a free crack": *Admiral Halsey's Story*, 217.
149   "Form Leo": Third Fleet action report; Adm. Arleigh Burke, oral history.
150   "We estimate enemy could be": Third Fleet action report.
150   "our surface forces now engaging": Ibid.

151   "I have the target in sight": *Essex* action report, dated November 22, 1944.

151   "The destroyers below are firing at us": Ibid.

151   "let go with his main batteries": Ibid.

152   "Sprague under fire . . . request immediate strike": Third Fleet action report.

152   "When an opportunity presents itself": Ibid.

152   "When I get my teeth": Marshall, "Wartime Experiences," 71.

14. ROUT OF THE JAPANESE CARRIERS

162   "swallowed a good deal of salt water": Air Group 9 action report.

163   "Instruct pilots to attack undamaged ships": Third Fleet action report.

164   "presented a picture of wild confusion": *Lexington* action report.

15. PURSUIT

167   "The pursuit phase": Third Fleet action report.

167   "sustained strikes": Ibid.

168   "Listen for contacts": Quoted in Morison, *History of U.S. Naval Operations in World War II*, 12:310.

168   "swung around . . . to make an anvil attack": *Hancock*'s Torpedo Squadron 3 action report.

170   Don't-tread-on-me dispatch: Third Fleet action report.

171   "Currently our carrier air groups are being debilitated": Task Force 38 action report.

173   "shoot them down in a friendly sort of way": *Admiral Halsey's Story*, 272.

AFTERWORD

176   "Admiral, you made a big mistake": *Admiral Halsey's Story*, 226.

177   "Attack Repeat Attack": Ibid., 121.

177   "Let others tell the story": Carney oral history.

BIBLIOGRAPHICAL ESSAY

Although an "I was there" memoir, this volume is closely based on action reports of the commands and ships involved in 1944 in the battle for Leyte. All such reports are still to be found at the Naval Historical Center in the Washington Navy Yard. I also drew on a wonderful resource, the exhaustive though unfinished five-volume *Strategic and Tactical Analysis* of the battle, by Commo. Richard Bates at the Naval War College at Newport, now available also at the Naval Historical Center. This study examines all planning and combat dispatches to arrive at what each commander knew each time he issued or received an order. The Leyte volume of Samuel Eliot Morison's standard *History of U.S. Naval Operations in World War II* (Boston: Little Brown, 1958) is largely based upon this work.

As to our Third Fleet chieftain, I also consulted the document he dictated after war's end, and on which the book *Admiral Halsey's Story* (New York: McGraw-Hill, 1947) is based, on file at the Virginia Historical Society. This, too, is now available at the Naval Historical Center. In addition I found useful correspondence in the Halsey Papers at the Library of Congress. Of the several biographies of the admiral, the latest, best, and most nearly authoritative is Prof. E. B. Potter's *Bull Halsey* (Annapolis, Md.: Naval Institute Press, 1985.)

Many of Halsey's commanders have written or been the subject of books, and others have left important oral histories, notably admirals Arleigh Burke and Gerald Bogan. To my knowledge, no member of Halsey's staff has written about Leyte. Of recollections and incidental papers, I have made most use of my old friend and colleague John Fellows Marshall's 97-page mimeo manuscript "Wartime Experiences" (1974; revised and privately printed as *Civilian in Uniform*, 1994). I have benefited from letters from and interviews with the following, many now dead: Guillaem Aertsen, Edward McC. Blair, Robert L. Balfour, Irwin E. Blum, Robert B. Brady, Joe Bryan, Thomas B. Buell, Taylor F. Caldwell, Robert B. Carney, Bladon Claggett Jr., Charles C. Colt, Molly C. Cox, Brenda Cheek, J. Donald Dunn, Thomas H. Dyer, Henry E. Eccles, Richard W. Emory, John P. English, James H. Flatley III, Charles M. Fox Jr., A. Kennie Gifford, Burton J. Goldstein, John Goodbody, William H. Halsey III, H. L. Hoerner, W. J. Holmes, Albert E. Jarrell, C. M. Kirkeeng, John E. Lawrence, C. E. Lile, John F. Marshall, David McClintock, William McMillan, A. H. McCollum, Redfield Mason, Standish Massie, James Merrill, H. D. Moulton, E. C. Outlaw, William Phelps, Roger Pineau, Robert B. Pirie, Will Player, Gordon Prange, Sigurd Rishovd, Ernest L. Schwab, R. J. Selmer, Gilvin Slonim, Harold Stassen, Raymond W. Thompson, T. C. Tillar, John Wilmerding, Ralph E. Wilson, and Hugh Winters. Of these, twenty-three were members of Third Fleet staff in October 1944.

Recalling life aboard Halsey's flagship I consulted Siegfried Dreyer's *Battleships and Battle Cruisers, 1905–70* (Garden City, N.Y.: Doubleday, 1973); Robert Dorr's *The "New Jersey": The Navy's Big Guns* (Osceola, Wis.: Motorbooks International Publishers, 1988); Ivan Musicant's *Battleship at War: The Epic Story of the USS Washington* (New York: Harcourt Brace Jovanovich, 1986); Malcolm Muir's *Iowa*-Class Battleships (Poole, Dorsetshire, England: Blandford Press, 1987); and Alan F. Pater's *U.S. Battleships: History of America's Greatest Fighting Fleet* (Beverly Hills, Calif.: Monitor Book Co., 1968). As to carriers I looked to Norman Polmar's *Aircraft Carriers* (Garden City, N.Y.: Doubleday, 1969), and Norman Friedman's *Aircraft Carriers* (Annapolis, Md.: Naval Institute Press, 1983), but turned most often to J. Bryan III's *Aircraft Carrier* (New York: Ballantine Books, 1954). On submarines, the record is set forth in Theodore Roscoe's *U.S. Submarine Operations in World War II* (Annapolis, Md.: Naval Institute Press, 1949), but I favored the incomparable War Patrol reports of combat submarines, accessible at the Naval Historical Center.

Finally, this memoir hung fire for years as I groped for the document I remembered in Harris Cox's hands on the night of October 24, 1944, fruitlessly ransacking JICPOA and ONI bulletins and Seventh Fleet reports, even missing the clues in Jasper Holmes's memoir of Pacific intelligence, *Double-edged Secrets* (Annapolis, Md.: Naval Institute Press, 1975). Then one day last year, as I talked with archivist Mike Walker at the Naval Historical Center, Jane Tucker overheard my effort to describe the lost paper. A talented, young Japanese-language specialist researching a war documentary for Japanese television, she could help a superannuated seeker. Recently, she told me, she had seen the paper I was looking for. It was, she said, a captured document translated at General MacArthur's headquarters, and I could find a copy at the National Archives in Suitland, Maryland. One look next morning at that copy of Admiral Koga's Z-Plan, and I recognized at once the long-sought paper — the catalyzing document for this memoir. Its title: "Allied Translator and Interpreter Section, Southwest Pacific Area, No. 4, dated 23 May 1944: 'Z' Operation Orders." The MacArthur Memorial archive in Norfolk also has a copy.

INDEX

Gifford, Kennie, 83
Goldstein, Burton J., 33, 154
Graham, William, 6
Green Island, 9
Grumman Avenger (TBF), 43, 59, 103–6, 126, 134–35, 139, 140, 156, 163, 168
Grumman Hellcat (F6F), 43, 46, 48, 50, 52, 55, 56, 59, 97, 98, 101, 102, 104, 105, 111, 159, 161, 162, 165
Grumman Wildcat (F4F), 35, 42, 43, 134, 138–40
Guadalcanal, 3, 4, 6, 12, 18, 19, 35, 36, 41, 73, 78, 81, 129, 152
Guam, 15, 118, 122, 158
Guerrillas, 12, 40
Guitarro, USS, 96, 97

Haddock, USS, 72
Halsey, William F., 6, 26, 51, 53, 64, 65, 68, 70, 75–82, 84, 95, 110–14, 122, 135, 148, 172, 174, 175; appearance of, 39, 40; "attack rpt attack," 104, 176; and Carney, 81; and carrier battle, 160, 163, 166; command style and strategy of, 8, 14, 23, 27, 37, 38, 55, 56, 63–65, 78, 79, 82–84, 104, 113, 126, 152–53, 167, 170–72; and decision at Leyte, 116–18, 120, 123, 125; as destroyerman, 39; early exploits of, 48, 158; and Formosa, 56–65; improvisational planning of, 22, 23, 64; and MacArthur, 6, 8, 28, 80; on flagship *Missouri,* 16, 173; and Nimitz directive, 15, 16; goes north, 149; and pilots, 70, 172; "retiring toward enemy," 65; goes to sea, 7, 14; "shoot them down in friendly way," 173; and submarines, 65, 75–77; and TF, 34, 17, 115, 152, 154–57, 163; v. First Striking Force, 95, 98–101, 103, 107, 108, 111, 115; and Yamamoto, 35–37

Hancock, USS, 62, 81, 165
Haruna, 181
Hawaii, 12, 15, 35, 63, 74, 100, 153, 158, 161, 176
Hayler, R. W., 129, 131, 132
Heermann, USS, 137
Henderson Field, 4, 18
Hibuson Island, 129, 132
Hickam Field, 13
Hoel, USS, 137
Hoerner, Herbert L. (Jack), 117
Hokkaido, 61
Hollandia, 12, 28, 42
Holmes, W. J., 121
Honolulu, 13, 72, 174
Honshu, 56, 61
Hornet, USS, 41, 42, 44, 49, 51, 155
Hull, Cordell, 31
Hull, USS, 25
Hustad, Carl, 6
Hutchins, USS, 151
Hyuga, 181

I-7, 75
I-19, 75
Icefish, USS, 77
Identification Friend or Foe (IFF), 50
Independence, USS, 43, 55, 95, 97, 104, 124–26
Indian Ocean, 122
Inland Sea, 76, 77, 110
Intelligence, 3, 5, 10, 30–38, 175–76
Intrepid, USS, 40, 99, 104, 147, 148, 162
Iowa, USS, 17, 18, 21, 24, 26, 104, 156, 157
Ise, 160, 180, 181
Island-hopping, 9, 10, 16, 127

Jacobs, Fenno, 48
Jallao, USS, 166, 167
Jeep carriers. *See* Escort carriers
Jellicoe, John B., 172

Pennsylvania, USS, 131
Pepper, George, 7
Pescadores Islands, 59, 77, 96
Petrof Bay, USS, 146
Philippine Islands, 5, 11, 13–15, 17, 28,
39, 40, 42, 50–55, 63–66, 68, 69, 75,
78–82, 84, 95–100, 103, 110, 115–17,
121, 122, 125, 127, 142, 153, 159, 160,
167
Philippine Sea, battle of the, 15, 25, 176
Phillips, R. H., 130
Photographic intelligence, 8, 12, 13, 27,
29, 33, 37, 161
Pintado, USS, 166
Plan Position Indicator (PPI), 50–51
Pope, A. J., 62
"Pope's Line," 4, 6, 11, 127
Porter, Frank, 8, 9
Powers, William, 20
Prince of Wales, HMS, 56, 57
Princeton, USS, 43, 101, 106, 111, 112,
114, 146, 171, 179, 180
Prisoner interrogation, 38

Quebec, summit at, 54

Rabaul, 4, 6, 8, 9, 35, 36, 120
Radar, 19, 24, 49, 51, 57, 60, 69, 70,
86, 97, 101, 111, 129, 147, 149, 150,
151, 157, 163; fire control, 19, 131, 164
Radio discipline, 42, 50
Radio intelligence, 5, 10, 110, 118;
direction-finding, 32; and traffic
analysis, 32
Radio Tokyo, 61, 65
Ransom, Robert, 107
Reagan, Francis, 23
Reconnaissance, carrier-based, 111, 112,
116; land-based, 13, 96, 110; night,
95, 124–25, 149, 153
Remey, USS, 130
Rennel Island, 58
Reno, USS, 63

Replacement aircraft, 48
Replacement pilots, 23–25, 43, 48, 79,
81, 82, 110, 159
Repulse, HMS, 56, 57
Riley, William E., 28, 54, 78, 118
Roberts, C. O., 164
Robinson, Charles A., 23
Rock, USS, 94
Ronquil, USS, 76
Roosevelt, Franklin D., 18, 31, 54, 65
Roper, Albert J., 61
Royal Air Force, 4, 5
Rushing, Kenneth, 102
Russell Islands, 35

St. Lo, USS, 144–45
Saipan, 15, 95, 110, 118, 122, 153
Salamaua, 12
Samar Island, 54, 75, 107, 114, 134, 135,
143, 151, 167, 168, 180
Sampson, W. T., 173
Samuel B. Roberts, USS, 137
Samurai, 143, 144
San Bernardino strait, 83, 84, 99, 101,
114, 115, 118, 124, 126, 128, 135, 140,
141, 151, 152, 155, 156, 167, 170–72,
176, 180
Sangamon, USS, 145–46
San Jacinto, USS, 61, 63, 147, 162, 164
Santa Cruz, battle of, 26, 42
Santee, USS, 145
Saratoga, USS, 42, 44, 75
Savo Island, 18, 19, 78, 82, 121
Schley, W. S., 173
Schwab, Ernest, 86, 94
Seadragon, USS, 77, 78, 90, 96
Semirara Island, 169
Seventh Fleet, 13, 75, 79, 96, 100, 119,
128, 134, 153, 154, 171, 172
Seventh Fleet intelligence center, 13
Shanghai, 58
Shark, USS, 73, 77, 78
Sherman, Forrest P., 28

About the Author

CARL SOLBERG joined the U.S. Naval Reserve as a second class seaman in 1942 and left active duty as a lieutenant in 1945, having served as an air combat intelligence officer with Admiral Halsey's Third Fleet. He began writing for *Time* as a cub reporter in 1939 after graduating from college and earning an M.A. and B.Litt. from Oxford University. He remained with the magazine until 1970, when he retired as an associate editor.

Solberg is the author of *Hubert Humphrey: A Biography, Conquest of the Skies: A History of Commercial Aviation in America, Riding High: America in the Cold War,* and *Oil Power.*

A native of Minneapolis, Minnesota, he now lives in Port Chester, New York, and is president of a scholarship-granting foundation in New York City.

THE NAVAL INSTITUTE PRESS IS THE BOOK-PUBLISHING ARM OF THE U.S. Naval Institute, a private, nonprofit society for sea service professionals and others who share an interest in naval and maritime affairs. Established in 1873 at the U.S. Naval Academy in Annapolis, Maryland, where its offices remain, today the Naval Institute has more than 100,000 members worldwide.

Members of the Naval Institute receive the influential monthly magazine *Proceedings* and discounts on fine nautical prints and on ship and aircraft photos. They also have access to the transcripts of the Institute's Oral History Program and get discounted admission to any of the Institute-sponsored seminars offered around the country.

The Naval Institute also publishes *Naval History* magazine. This colorful bimonthly is filled with entertaining and thought-provoking articles, first-person reminiscences, and dramatic art and photography. Members receive a discount on *Naval History* subscriptions.

The Naval Institute's book-publishing program, begun in 1898 with basic guides to naval practices, has broadened its scope in recent years to include books of more general interest. Now the Naval Institute Press publishes more than seventy titles each year, ranging from how-to books on boating and navigation to battle histories, biographies, ship and aircraft guides, and novels. Institute members receive discounts on the Press's nearly 400 books in print.

For a free catalog describing the Naval Institute Press books currently available, and for further information about subscribing to *Naval History* magazine or about joining the U.S. Naval Institute, please write to

Membership & Communications Department
U.S. Naval Institute
118 Maryland Avenue
Annapolis, Maryland 21402-5035

Or call, toll-free, (800) 233-USNI